Amos

SLAM BIDDING

by the same author

ADVANCED PLAY AT BRIDGE
HOW TO IMPROVE YOUR BRIDGE
KILLING DEFENCE AT BRIDGE
MORE KILLING DEFENCE AT BRIDGE
MATCH-POINT BRIDGE

Slam Bidding

H. W. KELSEY

FABER & FABER

3 Queen Square London

00024

First published in 1973
by Faber and Faber Limited
3 Queen Square London WC1
Printed in Great Britain by
Latimer Trend & Co Ltd Plymouth
All rights reserved

ISBN 0 571 10363 4

Acknowledgements

This time my list of benefactors is longer than usual. I am most grateful to Jack Marx for permission to publish, for the first time in book form, details of his Byzantine 4 NT convention, and to Bob and Jim Sharples for particulars of their slam-bidding methods.

I am indebted to Leon Sapire of Johannesburg for help with the chapter on asking bids and for permission to reproduce three hands from the Bridge Bulletin. My thanks are also due to Eric Milnes and Messrs. John Waddington for permission to use material from my articles and four hands from the Bidding Challenge feature in Bridge Magazine.

Finally, I owe a debt of gratitude to my proof readers, Denis Young and Tom Culbertson, whose stern and relentless criticism of the draft persuaded me to spend a great deal of time on revision.

H.W.K.

Contents

Introduction

Half the fun of this game of ours lies in bidding and making slam contracts. Everyone likes to bid slams, but those who do not keep careful records can have little idea whether they show a profit or a loss on their slam bidding.

The truth is that most players would be better off if they attempted no slams at all. Haphazard bidding methods, faulty judgement and a lack of discipline combine to produce this state of affairs. Points are lost in two ways, by missing good slams and by bidding bad ones.

At rubber bridge the loss is felt in the pocket, but apart from tightening up his judgement and self-discipline there is little that the rubber bridge player can do about it. Real precision in slam bidding is beyond the reach of casual partnerships.

In the tournament game it is another matter, since each player faces the partner of his choice. The degree of partnership understanding that can be achieved is limited only by the amount of time the players are prepared to devote to working on their bidding methods.

Attitudes are slowly changing. Thirty-five years ago Richard Lederer wrote: "Slam bidding is the most thrilling aspect of competitive duplicate. It is also the least important." Lederer's theory was that any team could be expected to chuck at least five thousand points in the course of a 32-board match and that the slam hands would not prove decisive.

This may have been true in Lederer's time but I doubt if it is today. Standards of bidding and play have improved to such an extent that one cannot rely on gains in the part-score and game department to offset losses in the slam zone. It has been calculated that there is a play for a slam on roughly one deal out of ten. That amounts to three or four potential slam swings in the course of a match, and no team can afford to be on the wrong side of them.

Perhaps influenced by Lederer's philosophy, the British and American system-makers of the 'thirties assigned a low priority to slam bidding, concentrating on what at that time seemed the more vital problems of constructive and competitive part-score and game bidding. The fruits of this policy have had a bitter taste in recent years. From the continent of Europe and particularly from Italy came exciting new variations on the one-club theme which made provision for the accurate investigation of slams.

Nobody is likely to dispute the fact that superior slam bidding has played a significant part in the domination of the world bridge scene by Italy in the past decade and a half. It is not the whole story, for in the Blue Team, Italy has a group of outstanding players welded together by a magnificent team spirit. Nevertheless, accurate slam bidding has been an important factor in their success.

If British and American players are to compete on equal terms, the time has come for a shift of emphasis. We must renovate our slam-bidding methods and bring them to a higher peak of efficiency. The tools are already in our possession for the most part, and those that are not can be borrowed from other systems. The greatest need is for players sufficiently disciplined and dedicated to put the machinery to proper use—players willing to spend long hours ironing out problems in advance and thus avoiding the partnership misunderstandings that are such a sad source of loss in international matches.

This book is written primarily for the keen tournament player in the hope that it will help him to bid more good slams and stay out of more bad ones.

The book divides naturally into two halves. The first six chapters are devoted mainly to a study of traditional methods. In addition to reviewing familiar ground, I have introduced one or two new ideas and turned the spotlight on some lesser-known conventions that seem worth while. Natural and well-tried methods predominate in the first half of the book, however, artificial sequences being the exception rather than the rule.

In the second half of the book we enter the realm of advanced slam bidding and the sequences become more complex. From a study of the brilliant intricacies of Byzantine we go on to examine the merits of asking bids of all kinds and the formidable and highly-specialised slam-bidding methods of the Roman, Precision and Blue Club systems. Those allergic to codified sequences may prefer to skim through some of the later chapters, reading just enough to keep them in touch with what is going on. It can be useful to have some idea of what the other man is playing even if you have no intention of playing it yourself.

My own preferences are clearly stated but I have tried to present a fair case for those methods which I do not favour, acting at times as devil's advocate in the process. Inevitably there will be many who disagree with my conclusions. This does not worry me, for my intention is not to persuade others to my way of thinking, but to display a wide range of slam-bidding aids from which the reader can select his own "best buy".

1 · General Principles

In a book concerned with the mechanics of slam bidding it is fitting to start with a definition. What is meant by successful slam bidding?

It is best defined as that which can be expected to show a clear profit on balance. Players can be satisfied with their slam bidding when the number of good slams they bid exceeds the combined total of good slams missed and bad slams bid. This immediately leads to a supplementary question. What is meant by a good slam?

The arithmetic of the subject is simple. When you bid a non-vulnerable small slam in a major suit and go one down, you lose 50 points where you might have gained 450—a total loss of 500. When the slam succeeds you gain the slam bonus, which is also 500. Vulnerable you risk the loss of 750 against the possible gain of 750. It follows that a small slam is a reasonable proposition if it is as likely to succeed as to fail. Any slam offering better than a fifty-fifty chance of success is a good slam and should be bid.

A small slam depending on no more than a 3-2 break is thus a very good slam, while one depending on a finesse and nothing else is a borderline case. A slam requiring a successful finesse *and* a 3-2 break is little better than a one in three chance and should not be bid. If you need a 3-2 break and one out of two finesses you are just on the right side of the odds with 51%. In practice it is hard to estimate these chances during the course of the bidding, and you will often be uncertain as to whether or not you are in a good slam until dummy goes down. An extra knave in partner's hand may do away with the need for a 3-2 break, while a helpful lead may enable you to avoid a finesse.

Some players declare themselves perfectly willing to play in slam when they have everything except the ace and king of a side suit. They call this a "three to one shot" on the theory that the defender on lead will not attack the weak suit unless he holds both ace and king. That may be carrying matters a little too far, but there is no doubt that the possibility of a favourable lead adds an appreciable if incalculable percentage to the chances of success.

When it comes to grand slams the odds are not so good. Now you are risking the game and small slam bonuses against the prospect of the grand slam bonus. If not vulnerable you risk 1000 for the gain of 500, if vulnerable 1500 for the gain of 750. Clearly a grand slam is not worth bidding unless it can be expected to succeed twice as often as it fails. A grand slam depending on a 3-2 break is thus no better than a fair proposition.

In the pairs game you require better odds than this unless you happen to be desperate for tops. Bidding and making a small slam normally produces a good enough score, and it is unwise to attempt a grand slam without odds of about four to one in your favour.

It is at international match point scoring that grand slams can be bid most freely, and of course this is the method of scoring now used in most team events. The i.m.p. scale reduces the effect of large swings, so that in bidding a grand slam you are risking 14 i.m.p. to gain 11 when not vulnerable and 17 to gain 13 when vulnerable. This makes the break-even point for bidding a grand slam about 57%.

In theory a grand slam that depends on one of two suits breaking 3-3 is just worth bidding, but in practice experienced players insist on better odds. After all, the above figures are predicated on the assumption that the small slam will be bid at the other table. If the opponents stop in game you are clearly backing a loser in attempting a grand slam, risking 22 i.m.p. for the sake of an extra 3 when not vulnerable, 26 i.m.p. for an extra 4 when vulnerable. It is therefore advisable to have a little surplus percentage in your favour. Let us say that at i.m.p. scoring a grand slam should have at least a 60% chance of success before it can be considered a good slam.

As a first step towards improving your slam bidding, I suggest that you keep records with a view to discovering just how good or bad it is at present. Use a page from your notebook or diary, draw a line down the middle, and after each session jot down the number of good slams bid on one side, the number of good slams missed and bad slams bid on the other. Remember to go by the expectancy of success rather than the actual result on the hand. A good slam is still good even if in practice it is defeated by an unlucky break. And a bad slam remains bad whether you get away with it or not.

If you keep careful records over a period of six months or longer, the accumulated evidence may jolt you into taking a hard look at your slam-bidding technique.

What Makes a Slam?

The recipe for a successful small slam contains two main ingredients.

1. Power. The combined hands must contain sufficient power to generate twelve tricks in one way or another. On balanced hands this power will normally consist of at least 33 high-card points. On distributional hands the long suits may provide playing tricks to make up for a deficiency of high-card points.

2. Controls. The hands must contain enough controls to ensure that the opponents cannot cash two tricks before you can develop your twelve. The obvious minimum requirement for a small slam is first-round control (ace or void) in three suits and second-round control (king or singleton) in the fourth.

Of these two vital ingredients power is the more important. A favourable lead may allow you to get away with a slam when the control position is insecure, but there is little hope if you are short of the power required to develop twelve tricks.

If it is intended to play in a suit contract, a further requirement is a solid or near-solid trump suit. It may well be possible to dispose of a loser in an outside suit, but trump losers are inescapable. A loser in the trump suit can be tolerated only when there are no losers elsewhere. A trump suit that would be quite adequate at the game level, such as A 10 x x opposite J x x x, is therefore pretty hopeless for slam purposes.

Before making any move towards slam, a player must be satisfied that there is a good strain in which to play. If a trump suit has not been agreed, or if there is doubt about the quality of the trumps, he must feel confident that the hand will play well in no trumps.

The first indication that a slam may be on the cards arises when a player becomes conscious of a surplus of power in the combined hands. This awareness may come about as early as the first round of bidding, and it is all the better if it does. When partner opens with a forcing bid of two clubs and you have useful values in your own hand, for instance, you will immediately be aware of slam possibilities. If you open a better-than-minimum hand and hear a jump shift from partner, you will again realise that you are close to the slam zone in potential.

At other times the presence of surplus power will not be disclosed until the second round of bidding, at which stage it is desirable for at least one of the partners to reveal the full strength of his hand. For slam purposes, the earlier the presence of surplus power is detected, the better, for this allows more time to agree a trump suit and check up on controls.

This brings us to some matters of system that need to be discussed before we can proceed further.

Two-Club Versus One-Club Systems

It is probably true to say that nine out of ten tournament players in the world today use some variation of either a one-club or a two-club system of bidding. The latter are generally claimed to be "natural" systems, although it is a little hard to understand why a forcing bid of one club should be considered less natural than a forcing bid of two clubs.

Since Culbertson's strong two bids went out of fashion in the nineteen-fifties, most tournament players in the United States have used two clubs as their forcing bid. In Britain two-club systems predominate, with Acol by far the most popular, while canapé-style systems incorporating a forcing bid of two clubs, are widely played on the continent of Europe.

The last decade, however, has been marked by a resurgence of one-club systems, which have gained ground all over the world. Little-club systems such as Roman have their devotees, but the ones that have really fired the public imagination are the modern big-club systems, Blue Club and Precision.

In the big-club systems the artificial forcing bid of one club guarantees a minimum of 17 points (16 in the case of Precision). Some allow natural responses to one club while others specify control-showing responses. No matter which method of responding is used, the effect is to keep the bidding low on big hands, disclosing surplus power at an early stage and allowing plenty of room for detailed slam investigation.

The big-club systems enjoy a further advantage in that their opening bids of one diamond, one heart and one spade are by definition limited to less than 17 points. The narrow range for one-bids other than clubs makes it easy for the opening bidder to express his full values on the second round without fear of being carried overboard by his partner.

Whether these advantages fully compensate for the clumsiness of the one-club systems in dealing with hands containing club suits is another matter and one which I do not propose to discuss here. My purpose in writing this book is not to prove that one system is superior to another. In general I believe that it does not much matter which system you adopt—it is how you play it that counts.

We shall examine slam bidding from within the structure of a two-club system, but I intend to have a look at the slam-bidding methods of other systems to see what can be borrowed for use within our framework. There is no reason why we should remain faithful to traditional methods that have proved themselves of dubious worth. Any system that cannot absorb new ideas and adapt itself to modern conditions will not remain long in the forefront.

Good slam bidding derives from a sound basic method, irrespective of the system used. Since an opening two-bid is often the springboard for a slam, we had better take a brief look at the schedule of two-bids that will be used as a base for the bidding sequences in the first half of the book.

2 ♣ — Forcing to game (with minor exceptions).
2 ♦ — Roman (5-4-4-0, 16-20 or 4-4-4-1, 17-21).
2 ♥ ⎫
2 ♠ ⎬— Acol. Powerful hand with eight playing tricks.
2 NT — Balanced hand with 20-22 points.

The Roman two diamond opening bid is an example of a convention originating in a one-club system which has been successfully adopted by many players of two-club systems throughout the world. Although its frequency of occurrence is not high (about 0.35% which is similar to that of the two-club opening bid) the manner in which it facilitates the bidding of

B

distributional games and slams makes it worth its place. The Blue Club variations on the Roman two diamond theme are discussed in detail in a later chapter.

One of the problems in playing a two-club system is the wide range of the opening bid of one in a suit. This is partly overcome by the use of Acol two-bids, or some other type of intermediate two-bids, in the major suits. Acol two-bids also have a relatively low frequency of occurrence, but by removing the eight-playing-trick hand from the range of one-bids they exert a beneficial effect on the whole field of constructive bidding and confer some of the advantages of a one-club system.

Many players, particularly in the United States, prefer to use weak two-bids in the major suits. This is a playable method that has certain obvious advantages, but it has the drawback of leaving the opening bid of one in a suit to cover a range of from 12 to 22 points, which is too wide for comfort.

It is, of course, possible to play both weak and Acol two-bids by using the convention originated by Albert Benjamin of Glasgow. Playing Benjamin, the opening bids of two spades and two hearts are weak, two diamonds is the game force with a two-heart negative, and two clubs shows an Acol two-bid in any of the four suits, the suit being named on the next round. Every convention has its price, however, and you cannot play Benjamin and retain the Roman two diamonds.

Perhaps the best solution for those who wish to play weak two-bids in the majors is the Kaplan-Sheinwold idea of reducing slightly the requirements for an opening bid of two clubs, admitting non-forcing sequences not only after a two no trump rebid but also when the opener bids and rebids the same suit at minimum level. We shall examine this idea more closely in a later chapter.

The Jump Shift

Now we come to a question that many will consider to be simply a matter of style. What sort of hand should the responder hold to justify a jump shift or forcing takeout? It may be a matter of style, but is a matter so vital that the success or failure of your slam-bidding methods is likely to depend upon how you play it.

In Britain and on the continent of Europe the tendency is to jump whenever game is assured unless there is considerable doubt about the final denomination. There are great advantages in this style. Although the jump shift is forcing only to game, the early indication of surplus power alerts partner at once to any slam possibilities there may be in the hand. And once the responder has got the hand off his chest with a jump shift he can afford to relax, contenting himself with minimum bids on subsequent rounds and leaving further initiative to his partner.

In Standard American, on the other hand, the jump shift denotes such a powerful hand that it is practically forcing to slam. Needless to say, this monster hardly ever turns up. With anything less than a real powerhouse, Standard American players are expected to institute a slow crawl towards game, using methods involving so many forcing sequences that it becomes hard to find a spot where the bidding may be dropped at all. Many American writers have pointed out the folly of this practice, but it is only in recent years that a trend towards a lighter jump shift has been discernible.

There are three types of hand on which the jump shift can profitably be employed.

(1) Balanced hands of 16 points or more.
(2) Strong hands with a good independent suit.
(3) Strong hands with four-card or better support for partner's suit.

Here are some examples of the three types.

(1) ♠ A K 7 4
♡ 9 3
♢ A J 3
♣ A 10 8 2

When partner opens the bidding with one heart it is advisable to force to game immediately with a bid of two spades. Having passed the message that you have a good hand, you can relax and allow partner to determine the level of the final contract. If he rebids three clubs you will raise, of course, but if his rebid is two no trumps, three diamonds, three hearts or three spades you will simply bid three no trumps and leave the rest to him.

The danger in making a one-over-one response on this type of hand is that it may subsequently prove difficult, if not impossible, to show your full strength below the game level. Suppose you respond one spade and partner rebids two diamonds or two hearts. A jump to three no trumps at this stage would be a bit of an underbid, so you rebid three clubs. But what will you do if your partner now bids three no trumps? You have not come close to showing the full potential of your hand, and whatever you do may be wrong. You must either pass and risk missing a laydown slam, or make a further effort and chance going one down in four no trumps.

Trying to catch up after an initial underbid frequently has the effect of carrying you into the never-never territory between game and slam. And there is nothing that makes you appear more foolish than going one down in five of a major.

(2) ♠ 7 5
♡ A K Q 10 8 3
♢ A 6 2
♣ 6 5

This is the second type of hand on which an immediate jump shift is the best answer. Respond two hearts to an opening bid of one club or one diamond and three hearts to an opening bid of one spade and you will avoid later complications. No matter what the rebid is, you simply repeat your long suit and leave further action to partner.

Again there are problems if the jump shift is not used. Suppose you respond two hearts to one spade and partner rebids his spades. A jump to four hearts will not now express your full values, so perhaps you manufacture a further force by bidding three diamonds. After that anything can happen, but partner is certainly unlikely to have an accurate picture of your holding.

(3) ♠ 7
♡ Q J 5 2
♢ Q 6 2
♣ A K Q 8 5

The third type of hand on which an immediate jump shift is required is the powerful hand containing four-card or better support for partner's suit. In response to an opening bid of one heart, a jump to three clubs followed by minimum heart bids will give partner the picture and enable him to make an intelligent decision about slam prospects.

Responding two clubs and following with a jump to four hearts does not express accurately the power of the above hand. Holding ♠ 9 6, ♡ A K 10 6 3, ◇ A 8 7, ♣ J 3 2, partner would have no reason to make a further effort and a good slam would be missed.

In determining whether or not to make a jump shift with support for partner's suit, pay less attention to the point count than to power and controls. The following hand contains no more than 11 high-card points but is a perfectly good response of three clubs when partner opens one spade.

♠ K 10 8 7 3
♡ 9 6
◇ 2
♣ A K J 5 4

Many players prefer to use the delayed game raise on this type of hand, responding two clubs and following with a jump to four spades. This may work out all right if partner co-operates by rebidding two diamonds or two hearts, but if he repeats his spades the inference of big trump support is lost. Your jump to four spades then promises no more than three small trumps or perhaps a doubleton honour. What is partner expected to do with a minimum hand such as ♠ A J 9 6 5 2, ♡ A 7, ◇ Q 9 3, ♣ 8 3?

As a matter of fact the machinery of the delayed game raise can be thrown out of gear in several ways.

(1) If partner makes a minimum rebid in his suit.

(2) If partner reverses or makes some other strong bid.

(3) If the opponents intervene.

In each of the above eventualities the responder may find himself in considerable difficulty on the second round, bereft of any means of putting across the message of strong trump support.

The British International Trials of 1966 threw up a hand on which the delayed game raise proved ineffective in the face of competitive bidding.

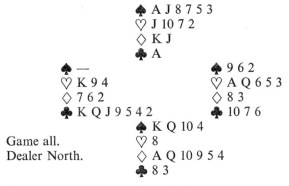

♠ A J 8 7 5 3
♡ J 10 7 2
◇ K J
♣ A

♠ —
♡ K 9 4
◇ 7 6 2
♣ K Q J 9 5 4 2

♠ 9 6 2
♡ A Q 6 5 3
◇ 8 3
♣ 10 7 6

♠ K Q 10 4
♡ 8
◇ A Q 10 9 5 4
♣ 8 3

Game all.
Dealer North.

The following was a typical bidding sequence.

W	N	E	S
	1♠	—	2◇
3♣	3♡	4♣	4♠
all pass			

South's raise to four spades might have been made on a much weaker trump holding and North could hardly proceed beyond game. The failure to jump immediately compelled South to choose on the second round between an underbid of four spades and an overbid of five spades.

At the three tables where South responded three diamonds on the first round the slam was reached in comfort.

The only type of strong hand on which it does not pay to jump on the first round is the two-suited or semi-two-suited hand lacking support for partner's suit.

♠ 7
♡ A K 9 8 5
◇ A J 10 3
♣ A 6 5

On this hand it would be unhelpful to force with three hearts in response to an opening bid of one spade. Here you are concerned not so much with telling partner about your big hand as with discovering the correct denomination, and that can best be achieved by going slowly. Rather than give information, you wish to receive information from partner about his strength and distribution. A simple response of two hearts, followed by three diamonds over two spades, will help to unearth any suit fit that exists.

After forcing with three hearts, you would have to start guessing over a rebid of three spades. Three no trumps could go down with six diamonds on, but a bid of four diamonds might carry you beyond the only makable contract.

Here is another hand on which an immediate jump shift is inadvisable.

♠ A 9 8 7 3
♡ K
◇ A Q
♣ K Q 7 4 2

The best response to an opening bid of one heart is a simple one spade. You have a powerful hand, but partner will need to support one of your suits or make a strong rebid before, you can start thinking about a slam. After responding one spade you can bid three clubs on the next round and hear a further natural rebid from partner.

The trouble with an immediate force of two spades is that you would probably feel obliged to bid your clubs at the four-level on the next round. But if the hand is a complete misfit three no trumps may be the only game that can be made.

Forcing Sequences

Many years ago Ely Culbertson pointed out that a forcing bid is a necessary evil. Modern players appear to see the necessity more readily than the evil, for the tendency is towards an ever-increasing use of artificial bids with more and more sequences defined as forcing.

It cannot be denied that forcing sequences are necessary, since there are many hands that cannot be bid accurately without them. This applies particularly to slams level, and in the remainder of this book a great deal of space is devoted to a study of specialised conventions and treatments involving the use of forcing bids.

In this chapter, however, I would like to point out the disadvantages of using forcing sequences in the early auction. By its nature a forcing bid is unlimited and does not make a full disclosure of strength. Partner is required to find another bid, but he is denied equal rights. Unable to estimate the combined strength of the hands, he is in no position to make an intelligent decision about the level of the final contract. All he can do is attempt to describe his hand further. This may work all right for a certain type of hand on which it is appropriate for one player to assume the captaincy and receive information without giving any in return. But it is not an ideal relationship for the majority of hands. A series of one-round forces in a slow, scientific auction keeps partner under constant pressure, and anyone subjected to pressure for long periods is liable to crack.

Limit Bids

A limit bid defines the strength of a hand fairly closely. Being by nature non-forcing, the limit bid has great advantages. In the first place it relieves partner of strain by telling him not only the truth about your hand, but also the whole truth. Armed with the knowledge of the combined strength of the two hands, partner can quickly assess the level at which you should play and take the appropriate action. Furthermore, if the bidding continues, the limit bidder can show features as freely as he pleases, secure in the knowledge that his hand remains limited and that his efforts cannot be misconstrued.

Players who appreciate the benefit of making life easy for their partners have no doubt that the most important of all bidding rules is to limit their hands at the first opportunity. When faced with a choice between two sound actions, a one-round force and a limit bid, they will choose the limit bid every time.

Suppose partner opens one diamond and you hold:

♠ K 9 4
♡ K J 3
◇ Q 7 6
♣ A J 7 3

The response of two clubs gives partner little useful information, but the limit bid of three no trumps tells the whole story and gets the hand off your chest.

♠ J 10 6 5
♡ K 10 5
◇ A Q 8 3
♣ 6 2

When partner opens one spade a response of two diamonds cannot be described as unsound. A limit raise to three spades gives a more accurate picture of the general strength, however.

The family of limit bids contains the following groups.

1. All natural no trump bids.

For most players the opening bid of one no trump has a three-point range, 12-14, 13-15, 15-17, or 16-18. The no trump opening used to be considered an ineffective springboard for slams, but with the advent of streamlined methods of locating a suit fit this is no longer the case.

The response of one no trump has a wider range, normally 6-9 points and occasionally 10. The range of a response in no trumps becomes narrower, however, as the bidding draws nearer to game. For those who use limit bids the jump response in no trumps, e.g. 1 ♠-2 NT, shows a balanced hand of 11-12 points, denying the ability to bid game. The jump rebid in no trumps, e.g. 1 ♡-1 ♠, 2 NT, also has a narrow range, showing 17-18 and denying the strength to bid three no trumps.

2. All natural raises.

The single raise of partner's suit has a comparatively wide range of 6-10 points including distribution. The double raise has a narrower range of 11-12 and denies the ability to bid game.

3. Rebids in the same suit.

A minimum rebid in the same suit by the opener limits his hand to no more than 14 points. With a stronger hand he will find a more encouraging rebid. The jump rebid, e.g. 1 ♡-1 ♠, 3 ♡, is limited to a hand containing seven playing tricks and invites game if the responder has extra values. The jump rebid by responder, e.g. 1 ♡-1 ♠, 2 ◊-3 ♠, is again merely invitational, denying the strength to bid game.

4. Preference bids.

A simple preference bid is limited by the failure to jump; a jump preference by the failure to bid game.

5. Pre-emptive bids.

All pre-emptive bids are strictly limited and the pre-emptor will not normally speak again.

Other non-forcing bids can be described as limited in a broader sense. The opening bid of one in a suit, for example, is limited in some measure by the failure to open with a two-bid. A simple change of suit by the opener is limited by his failure to make a stronger rebid. Even an opener's reverse, although showing a fair hand, is limited within a fairly narrow range.

In Britain, at any rate, many players treat the opener's reverse after a one-level response as non-forcing. West's hand is thus limited by his failure to force with a bid of three hearts, and East can pass with a sigh of relief.

The knowledge that partner will force to game by making a jump shift whenever he has the material to do so, lays a sound foundation for accurate slam bidding. On nine hands out of ten one of the partners will be able to disclose his full strength not later than the second round of bidding, whereupon it becomes easy to estimate the slam prospects.

It is in the slow, scientific auctions, full of inferential forces, but bereft of limit bids, that the players are liable to arrive at the game level still uncertain about the presence or absence of surplus power. This inevitably leads to a number of missed slams and ventures into that most futile of contracts, five of a major.

You will find, therefore, that the bidding sequences in the first half of this book follow the Acol style, making maximum use of limit bids in the early rounds and resorting to forcing bids only when there is no alternative. If this is not your style I trust you will bear with it.

Slams on Power Alone

Many slams can be bid, and ought to be bid, in direct fashion by a natural extension of game-bidding technique. When a player hears a quantitative statement of strength from his partner he may realise at once that the combined hands contain sufficient power to generate twelve tricks. If the control position seems satisfactory he may go straight to slam. Alternatively, he may make a slam suggestion which his partner will accept or reject, depending on whether or not he has more than a minimum for his previous bid.

Here are some examples of slam auctions that do not contain a forcing bid.

		W	E
♠ A J 7 6 5 3	♠ K 9 8 2	1 ♠	3 ♠
♡ A 4	♡ Q 10 6	6 ♠	—
♢ A K 8 4	♢ 7 2		
♣ 7	♣ K Q 9 4		

With good controls, West knows that any hand his partner can hold for his limit raise is likely to offer a play for twelve tricks. A grand slam, while not impossible from West's point of view, must be highly unlikely since East would need to hold specific cards. It does not pay to be too greedy. The chance of being able to locate the key cards for a grand slam by bidding all round the clock is heavily outweighed by the risk of indicating the best defence against six spades. West therefore goes straight to the small slam.

		W	E
♠ A Q 4	♠ 7 2	2 NT	4 NT
♡ K Q 6	♡ A J 9	6 NT	—
♢ K Q J 3	♢ 7 6 4		
♣ A 10 2	♣ K Q J 7 3		

The opening bid shows a balanced hand within the range of 20—22 high-card points. East responds with a limit raise, denying the values to bid six himself but suggesting a slam if the opening bid is better than a minimum. Holding 21 points and good controls, West accepts the try and bids the slam.

♠ A 8 7	♠ Q 6 4	*W*	*E*
♡ K Q 10 5 4	♡ J 3	1 ♡	2 NT
◇ A Q J 6 4	◇ K 9 5 2	6 ◇	—
♣ —	♣ A J 8 4		

Again West can tell that a small slam is probable and a grand highly unlikely. He therefore goes straight to six, offering his partner a choice of suit. There are many hands that East could have held on which the slam would have been unbeatable. On the actual cards the slam is at risk on a spade lead, but the spade lead would have been more marked if West had adopted a slow approach.

You will come across plenty of opponents who laugh at such blunt and unpolished slam sequences. Blush all the way to the bank if you must, but do not let anyone talk you out of using direct methods when you have the appropriate hand. The advantage of withholding information from the defenders occasionally makes it worth while taking a chance on the control position.

♠ A Q J 7 4	♠ K 2	*W*	*E*
♡ Q J 5	♡ K 10 9 6 4 3	1 ♠	2 ♡
◇ 6	◇ A J 4	4 ♡	6 ♡
♣ A Q 7 6	♣ 8 3		

West's raise to four hearts, showing the full value of his hand, provides a solid base for East's slam bid. East takes a chance on the club position with his eyes wide open. Either a pussy-footing three club bid by West (giving North a chance to double) or a diamond bid by East, could help the opponents to find the killing defence if one exists.

So much for the slams that can be bid on power alone. On most hands it is advisable to check on controls in order to make sure that the defenders cannot cash two quick winners, and that brings us to the next chapter.

2 · Controls by Numbers

Controls can be checked individually or in bulk. In this chapter we shall confine our attention to the latter method, taking a look at some of the many slam conventions designed to discover the number of aces and kings that are held by the partnership.

From the beginning it was inevitable that the bid of four no trumps should serve as the starting point for most conventional slam enquiries. By the time the surplus power needed for slam becomes apparent the bidding has often reached the game level, and the bid of four no trumps, fairly idle in a natural sense, stands ready for conventional use.

Ely Culbertson was the first to recognise and exploit this fact when in 1933 he published details of his 4-5 no trump convention. This is now obsolescent, even in Britain where it made the most impact, but it remains a sounder method of checking controls than many that came after it.

Culbertson 4-5 No Trump Convention

After agreeing trumps and satisfying himself that the combined strength puts the hand in the slam zone, a player may bid four no trumps if he holds:

(a) three aces, or
(b) two aces and the king of a suit bid by either partner.

The responses are as follows:
(1) With two aces, or with one ace and the kings of all bid suits —bid 5 NT.
(2) Lacking either an ace or the kings of all bid suits—sign off in five of the lowest bid suit (which may or may not be the trump suit).

(3) With an ace or void in an unbid suit and adequate extra values—bid five in that suit.

(4) With an ace in a bid suit, or with the kings of all bid suits—jump to six in the trump suit.

After a bid of 4 NT and a five-level response, a bid of 5 NT is a grand slam try showing that all the aces are held. The sign-off at the six-level is in the agreed trump suit, but the responder may show extra features below that level or bid the grand slam himself.

Modifications introduced by the early Acol theorists allow the responder a great deal of discretion when he holds one ace. If he feels that he has already shown his full values in the previous bidding, he need not show his ace in response to 4 NT but may sign off, giving the message that he does not fancy his hand for slam purposes. Nor need he feel absolutely bound to sign off when lacking an ace or all the bid kings. A five-level response other than the lowest bid suit is played as encouraging, usually but not invariably denoting possession of an ace somewhere in the hand. The general message is that the responder likes his hand in relation to his previous bidding.

The great advantage of the convention is that the 4 NT bidder gives information about aces and kings as well as receiving it. The concept of the bid king is particularly valuable, for the partners can so arrange their bidding that the possession of key kings can be confirmed or denied. The convention has the merit of giving full partnership rights to both players, allowing each to express an opinion about the advisability of bidding a slam. Not the least of the benefits is the negative inference that arises when one partner or the other fails to bid 4 NT. Furthermore, enemy interference over 4 NT becomes less of a hazard when both partners are in a position to take intelligent action. There are few slam conventions that offer such scope for judgement.

Perhaps that is one of the reasons why the Culbertson 4-5 never achieved mass popularity. Players who are lazy by nature, and disinclined to think too hard, naturally prefer a convention that offers less scope for the exercise of judgement. Others reject Culbertson because they dislike restrictions on their freedom of action. These players resent being unable to bid four no trumps when lacking the required number of aces.

In Britain the Culbertson 4-5 has had a longer run than elsewhere, but over the years the tendency in expert as well as ordinary club circles has been towards simpler, if less effective, methods.

A more recent convention that shared some of the features of the Culbertson 4-5, the Declarative-Interrogative 4 NT, has already suffered a similar fate. Developed as part of the Neapolitan Club system, the D.I. 4 NT was used in the middle of a series of cue-bids. As well as asking for additional controls, it promised two aces if the hand was unlimited and one if limited.

It was found, however, that there were hands on which it was desirable to use this general slam try without holding the required number of aces, and in the Blue Club system, which is a stream-lined version of Neapolitan, the declarative part of the D.I. 4 NT bid has been abandoned. We shall consider this more fully in a later chapter.

The Blackwood Convention

Less than a year after the appearance of the Culbertson 4-5, Easley Blackwood of Indianapolis published his 4 NT convention. The simplicity of the device captured the imagination of the bridge public, and within a few years it had attained the wide-spread popularity that it enjoys today. Millions of players all over the world use the Blackwood 4 NT convention and derive a great deal of pleasure from it. Whether they derive much profit is another matter.

Blackwood lays down no requirements for a bid of 4 NT. When either partner feels that a slam may be within reach he can bid 4 NT to check on controls. The responses are:

> 5 ♣ — no ace or four
> 5 ♢ — one ace
> 5 ♡ — two aces
> 5 ♠ — three aces

It used to be thought that there could be no possible ambiguity about the 5 ♣ response, until the following hand turned up in a World Championship match between France and Brazil at Taipei in 1971.

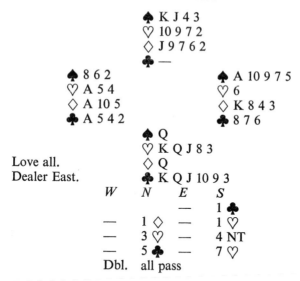

```
                    ♠ K J 4 3
                    ♡ 10 9 7 2
                    ◇ J 9 7 6 2
                    ♣ —
        ♠ 8 6 2                      ♠ A 10 9 7 5
        ♡ A 5 4                      ♡ 6
        ◇ A 10 5                     ◇ K 8 4 3
        ♣ A 5 4 2                    ♣ 8 7 6
                    ♠ Q
                    ♡ K Q J 8 3
Love all.           ◇ Q
Dealer East.        ♣ K Q J 10 9 3
        W       N       E       S
                        —       1 ♣
        —       1 ◇     —       1 ♡
        —       3 ♡     —       4 NT
        —       5 ♣     —       7 ♡
        Dbl.    all pass
```

The above was the electrifying bidding sequence when the French held the North-South cards. After North's jump to three hearts on the second round, which South considered to be forcing, South could not believe that the five club response showed no ace and therefore bid a hopeless grand slam.

In fairness it must be admitted, however, that by this stage the French team had already qualified for the final and were exercising an unfamiliar partnership.

If we keep that hand in mind as an awful warning, it is safe to claim that there will normally be no difficulty in deciding whether your partner is showing no ace or four aces when he responds five clubs to your Blackwood enquiry.

A subsequent bid of 5 NT by the 4 NT bidder guarantees that all four aces are held and invites the responder to bid the grand slam. If unable to do this he is expected to show his kings by a similar step schedule.

6 ♣ — no king
6 ♢ — one king
6 ♡ — two kings
6 ♠ — three kings
6 NT— four kings

Note that the response to show all four kings is 6 NT, not 6♣. There is no need for any degree of ambiguity at the six-level.

Blackwood is a simple convention, and a valuable one provided that its limits are recognised. It is a tool designed to keep players out of bad slams when two aces are missing, and it should be used only on a certain type of hand.

W	E		♠ K Q 10 8 6 5
1 ♣	2 ♠		♡ A K
3 ♠	?		♢ K Q 4 2
			♣ 7

In order to select the final contract, the only thing East needs to know is the number of aces held by West. A Blackwood bid of 4 NT is ideal.

Trouble arises when players regard Blackwood as the sole gateway to the slam zone. Blackwood is worse than useless when partner's response to 4 NT will still leave you uncertain of what to do. Consider the following hand.

W	E		♠ K 7
1 ♠	2 ♡		♡ K Q J 5 2
4 ♡	?		♢ 7 6 3
			♣ A 8 3

It is clear that you are close to the slam zone, but a quantitative check on aces will be of little use. Partner is not likely to have less than two aces, and if you employ Blackwood and hear a five heart response you will be no further forward. A slam bid will be a gamble, since partner may have either of the following hands.

(a)	♠ A Q J 6 4	(b)	♠ A Q J 6 4
	♡ A 9 8 3		♡ A 9 8 3
	♢ 9 5		♢ K Q
	♣ K Q		♣ 9 5

Blackwood cannot tell you about the two diamond losers in (a) or the twelve cold tricks in (b).

C

If partner shows three aces you are no better off. You can follow with 5 NT to ask for kings, but the response will leave you fumbling in the dark.

(c)	♠ A Q J 6 4	(d)	♠ A 9 8 6 4
	♡ A 9 8 3		♡ A 9 8 3
	◇ A		◇ A K
	♣ 9 5 4		♣ 9 5

On (c) the grand slam is practically a lay-down, while on (d) it is a poor proposition in spite of the presence of a king.

Blackwood is not the answer when the slam depends on a fit. A better method of dealing with this sort of hand will be discussed in the next chapter.

An obvious occasion to avoid the use of Blackwood is when your hand contains a void, for you will have no means of telling whether partner's ace coincides with your void suit or not.

Voids in Responder's Hand

There are three distinct ways in which the responder to a Blackwood enquiry can indicate a void in his hand, but none of them is completely satisfactory.

1. The method recommended by Easley Blackwood himself is to make the normal response but at the six-level instead of the five-level. Thus a response of 6 ♣ shows no aces and a void, 6 ◇ one ace and a void, and so on. Clearly the responder must exercise discretion, making these responses only if he is sure that his void is a useful one.

2. Bid 6 ♣ to show one ace and a void, 6◇ to show two aces and a void, etc. This method has the advantage of keeping the bidding lower and can therefore be used more frequently when a minor suit is trumps.

3. Bid 5 NT to show two aces and a void. With one ace and a void in a suit ranking below trumps, bid six in the void suit. With one ace and a void in a suit ranking above trumps, bid six in the trump suit. This variation gains in some cases by specifying the void.

When is 4 NT Natural?

This is a matter for detailed partnership discussion. Divergent opinions are held on the subject, and misunderstandings are bound to occur unless the meaning of 4 NT in every possible sequence is agreed in advance.

My personal inclination is to abide by the following simple rules.

A bid of 4 NT is Blackwood only when a suit has been agreed specifically or by inference. In all other cases it is natural.

A raise of partner's no trump bid, as in the following sequences, is, therefore, natural and quantitative.

W	E	W	E	W	E	W	E
1 NT	4 NT	1 ♣	3 NT	2 ♣	2 ♠	1 ♠	2 ♡
			4 NT	2 NT	4 NT	3 NT	4 NT

There is one exceptional situation, where what appears to be a no trump raise should be read as conventional. This occurs after a jump shift by responder, who may then lack the space to agree trumps below the game level.

e.g.	W	E		W	E
	1 ♡	3 ◇		1 ♠	3 ♡
	3 NT	4 NT		3 NT	4 NT

In the first case the responder may have a heart fit and be unable to agree the suit without limiting his hand. In the second sequence the responder may intend to play in either hearts or spades, being too strong merely to bid the suit at game level.

A jump to 4 NT after a suit bid is always conventional, normally agreeing the last-bid suit.

e.g.	W	E	W	E	W	E
	1 ♠	4 NT	1 ♡	3 ♣	1 ♣	2 ♠
			3 ◇	4 NT	3 ♣	4 NT

4 NT is a natural sign-off when the bidder has previously limited his hand in no trumps.

e.g.	W	E	W	E	W	E
	1 NT	3 ♡	2 NT	3 ♣	1 ♠	2 ♢
	3 NT	4 ♢	3 ♠	4 ♣	3 ♡	3 NT
	4 NT		4 NT		4 ♢	4 NT

Gerber 4 ♣

Another widely-used method of checking on aces is the 4 ♣ convention suggested in 1938 by John Gerber of Houston. The responses are in steps similar to the Blackwood schedule.

$$4 ♢ — \text{no ace or four}$$
$$4 ♡ — \text{one ace}$$
$$4 ♠ — \text{two aces}$$
$$4 \text{ NT}— \text{three aces}$$

The 4 ♣ bidder can then go on to ask for kings, using by agreement either the next suit up (excluding trumps) or 5 ♣ as the conventional bid for this purpose.

Gerber has the advantage of starting the enquiry for aces at a lower level, thus making it possible to settle at the four-level in the event of an unfavourable response. The advantage may be neutralised, however, by the difficulty in distinguishing between natural and conventional 4 ♣ bids.

Some players solve this problem by treating all 4 ♣ bids as Gerber. Some regard 4 ♣ as Gerber unless a genuine club bid has been made during the auction. A further group plays 4 ♣ as Gerber only when partner's last bid was in no trumps, while others use Gerber only as a jump over an opening no trump bid.

Used in a restricted sense, the convention combines well with Blackwood. Many players, who normally bid 4 NT to ask for aces, play "Gerber over no trumps".

Key-Card Blackwood

This is one of the many variations that have been introduced over the years in an attempt to improve on the Blackwood theme. Developed as a feature of the CAB system, Key-Card Blackwood recognises the vital importance of the king of trumps by treating it as a fifth ace. The responses to 4 NT thus become:

5 ♣	—	no ace or four
5 ♢	—	one ace or five
5 ♡	—	two aces
5 ♠	—	three aces

Cases in which trumps are agreed by inference need special care, since doubt about the agreed trump suit can lead to disaster. In order to avoid all ambiguity, CAB players use Key-Card Blackwood only when trumps have been agreed by a direct raise.

A subsequent bid of 5 NT asks for kings in the normal manner, but naturally the king of trumps is not shown a second time.

In the play-off match to decide the team to represent North America in the 1971 Bermuda Bowl, the following hand illustrated the value of Key-Card Blackwood.

♠ J 10 9 8	♠ Q 5 4 3 2	W	E
♡ 8 6	♡ A K Q 5	1 ♣	1 ♠
♢ A 7	♢ K Q 6	2 ♠	3 ♡
♣ A K J 6 2	♣ 7	4 ♠	4NT
		5 ♡	?

The bidding was the same in both rooms up to this point. One pair was playing straight Blackwood and East had a difficult decision to make. He took the optimistic view that his partner was likely to have the king of trumps and bid the slam, but it was not his lucky day.

In the other room East and West were using Key-Card Blackwood, and East knew from the five heart response that either two aces or one ace and the king of trumps were missing. He therefore signed off in five spades and gained a big swing.

Norman 4 NT

This variation, originated by Sir Norman Bennet and Norman de Villiers Hart, asks for aces and kings to be shown together in one response. An ace is counted as one point and a king as half a point, and the schedule of responses is as follows:

5 ♣	—	less than 1½ points
5 ♢	—	1½ points
5 ♡	—	2 points
5 ♠	—	2½ points

5 NT — 3 points
6 ♣ — 3½ points
6 ◊ — 4 points
etc.

The Norman Convention has never achieved more than a limited popularity, although it was adopted enthusiastically by the Vienna System as its official 4 NT convention. Norman fits in well with the Culbertson asking bids and is still used by asking bidders in many parts of the world.

Basically, the idea of showing aces and kings together is sound. The Neapolitan System uses control-showing responses to the opening bid of one club on a very similar scale. At the five-level there is not too much room for manoeuvre, however, and Norman users have to take care lest the response to 4 NT carry them overboard.

One drawback of the convention is that an ace can be concealed in the 5 ♣ response, which may result in a missed slam. Furthermore, the 4 NT bidder will not invariably be able to identify the controls shown by his partner's response. For example:

♠ K Q 10 8 5	♠ A 9 7 4	W	E
♡ K Q J 5 2	♡ 8 4	1 ♠	3 ♠
◊ A Q	◊ K 9 5	4 NT	5 ♡
♣ 6	♣ K 8 7 3	?	

Now West wishes he were playing straight Blackwood, since the Norman 5 ♡ response does not tell him whether the slam is on or not.

Nevertheless Norman can be a real help when partner has the right cards.

♠ A	♠ K 8 2	W	E
♡ K 6 5	♡ A 7	1 ◊	3 ♣
◊ A K 9 4 3	◊ Q 6	4 ♣	4 NT
♣ K 6 4 2	♣ A Q J 10 7 3	6 ♣	7 NT

East can count thirteen tricks when he hears that all the aces and kings are present. After a Blackwood response of 5 ♡ East would hesitate to ask for kings for fear of receiving a 6 ◊ response.

Norman responses lend themselves readily to modification in two specific situations.

(1) When the partner of the 4 NT bidder has opened the bidding with a strong bid, three aces or the equivalent are then taken for granted and the schedule of responses becomes:

$$5 \clubsuit \quad - \quad \text{less than } 3\tfrac{1}{2} \text{ points}$$
$$5 \diamondsuit \quad - \quad 3\tfrac{1}{2}$$
$$5 \heartsuit \quad - \quad 4$$
$$5 \spadesuit \quad - \quad 4\tfrac{1}{2}$$
etc.

This schedule permits a large number of controls to be shown at a convenient level. For example:

♠ A J	♠ 7 6 4	W	E
♡ A 10 6 3	♡ K Q J	2 NT	3 ♣
◇ A K 8 5	◇ 6	3 ♡	4 ♣
♣ A J 3	♣ K Q 10 9 5 2	4 ◇	4 NT
		5 ♠	7 NT

Four aces and a king are all that East needs when he knows his partner to have a heart suit.

(2) The second modification is used when the responder has given a negative response to an opening forcing bid. This normally denies as much as an ace and a king, and the schedule of Norman responses becomes:

$$5 \clubsuit \quad - \quad \text{no more than one king}$$
$$5 \diamondsuit \quad - \quad \text{one ace}$$
$$5 \heartsuit \quad - \quad \text{two kings}$$

The above is the Vienna schedule, but since an ace is likely to be a more valuable holding than two kings there is a case for interchanging the 5 ◇ and 5 ♡ responses.

San Francisco 4 NT

This convention, which enjoys a limited popularity in the United States, represents another attempt to show aces and kings together. The valuation is different, however, an ace being counted as three points and a king as one. The step responses are as follows:

5 ♣	—	less than 3 points
5 ◇	—	3 points (A or KKK)
5 ♡	—	4 points (AK or KKKK)
5 ♠	—	5 points (AKK)
5 NT	—	6 points (AA or AKKK)
6 ♣	—	7 points (AAK or AKKKK)
etc.		

The effect of the 3:1 ratio is to remove ambiguity, making it easier for the 4 NT bidder to identify the exact cards shown by his partner's response.

The hand on page 38 that proved unsuitable for Norman is dealt with quite easily by San Francisco.

♠ K Q 10 8 5	♠ A 9 7 4	W	E
♡ K Q J 5 2	♡ 8 4	1 ♠	3 ♠
◇ A Q	◇ K 9 5	4 NT	5 ♠
♣ 6	♣ K 8 7 3	—	

Knowing from the response of 5 ♠ that two aces are missing, West is not tempted to go on.

However, the steep inclination of the scale of responses (going up by three steps for every ace held) means that great discretion is required of the San Francisco bidder if he is not to land too high. The response to show four aces, for instance, is 7 ♣, which clearly limits the application of the convention.

The disadvantage can be overcome to some extent by modifying the scale (starting perhaps at 9 points) when the partner of the 4 NT bidder has shown real strength.

Roman Blackwood

This convention has proved surprisingly popular with those seeking to improve on "steam" Blackwood. The original idea, incorporated in the Roman Club system, is to respond to 4 NT as follows:

5 ♣	—	no ace or three
5 ◇	—	one ace or four
5 ♡	—	two aces of the same colour or rank
5 ♠	—	two aces of different colour and rank

The idea of saving space by making the 5 ♣ and 5 ◇ responses serve a dual purpose made an instant appeal to many players. Although in theory there could be some ambiguity, in practice there is little difficulty. If in doubt after hearing a 5 ♣ or 5 ◇ response, the 4 NT bidder simply signs off at the five-level, relying on his partner to make another move if he has the stronger type of response.

It is the 5 ♡ and 5 ♠ responses that fulfil the main function of Roman Blackwood, enabling a player to bid 4 NT with a void in his hand and have a fair chance of identifying his partner's aces.

♠ K Q J 7 6 3		W	E
♡ —		2 ♠	3 ♣
◇ K Q J 10 5		3 ◇	4 ◇
♣ A K		4 NT	

Here a 5 ◇ response will not tell West whether the slam is on or not, but he will have odds of two to one in his favour if he bids it. A 5 ♡ response will positively identify the ace of hearts as one of the aces held (both major or both red), and West will know that six is the limit of the hand. But what West really wants to hear is a 5 ♠ response, for this enables him to bid the grand slam with confidence.

Sometimes the two-ace response will tell you when the grand slam is not on, but not when it is. Try interchanging the major suits in the above example.

♠ —		W	E
♡ K Q J 7 6 3		2 ♡	2 ♠
◇ K Q J 10 5		3 ◇	4 ◇
♣ A K		4 NT	

Now the 5 ♠ response tells West that the aces of spades and diamonds are held and he settles for six. But the 5 ♡ response brings frustration and leaves West with further work to do, since the grand slam may or may not be on.

A variation popular in Britain overcomes this problem by defining the two aces held more precisely.

> 5 ♡ — two aces of the same colour
> 5 ♠ — two aces of the same rank
> 5 NT — two aces of different colour and rank

When this variation is used, the 4 NT bidder who holds one

ace can always identify the two aces shown by his partner's response. He will occasionally be denied the chance to rebid 5 NT to ask for kings on the Roman schedule, but if it is thought worth while and if space permits 6 ♣ can be used for this purpose.

Many thinking players, while appreciating the value of the dual-purpose 5 ♣ and 5 ◇ responses, consider the Roman responses of 5 ♡, 5 ♠ and 5 NT to be wasted on trivial purposes. There are other ways of identifying aces opposite voids, as we shall see.

A variation that has some following in Europe is to use the 5 ♡ response to show two aces and not much else, and the 5 ♠ response to indicate two aces and extra values. Although a trifle vague, this is likely to be more useful information than the identity of the aces on nine hands out of ten.

Roman Gerber

This is a much more effective method of identifying controls. The initial responses to 4 ♣ follow Roman lines.

$$
\begin{array}{ll}
4 \diamondsuit & - \quad \text{no ace or three} \\
4 \heartsuit & - \quad \text{one ace or four} \\
4 \spadesuit & - \quad \text{two aces}
\end{array}
$$

The cheapest rebid by the 4 ♣ bidder (apart from the trump suit) now asks for kings on a similar schedule. If the 4 ♣ bidder skips a step, however, bidding the cheapest suit but one, he is asking for clarification of the previous response. With one ace the responder bids the suit, with three aces he bids the missing one, and with two aces he responds by steps as follows:

1st step — same colour
2nd step — different rank and colour
3rd step — same rank

At times it may be possible to identify specific kings. Here is an example.

♠ A Q J 10 7 3	♠ K 9 2	W	E
♡ A	♡ Q J 10 5 4	2 ♣	2 ♡
◇ A K	◇ J 7 3	2 ♠	3 ♠
♣ A Q 10 8	♣ K 3	4 ♣	4 ◇
		4 ♡	5 ♣
		5 ♡	5 ♠
		7 ♠	—

After trump agreement, West bids a Gerber 4 ♣ and is not surprised when his partner denies an ace. The cheapest rebid, 4 ♡, asks for kings and the response of 5 ♣ shows two. A bid of 5 ◇ from West at this stage would ask for queens. West is not interested in queens, however, and bids 5 ♡, skipping a step to ask for clarification of the king response. East's response of 5♠, showing kings of the same colour, makes the grand slam practically a laydown.

Opening 4 NT

The Acol idea of a conventional opening bid of 4 NT has been adopted by many other systems. The bid is used on those rare occasions when all that is needed for a slam is a particular ace in partner's hand. The responses are as follows:

5 ♣	—	no ace
5 ◇	—	ace of diamonds
5 ♡	—	ace of hearts
5 ♠	—	ace of spades
5 NT	—	two aces
6 ♣	—	ace of clubs

Here is a simple example.

♠ K Q J 10 9 5 3	♠ A	W	E
♡ —	♡ K Q J 10 9 7 5	4 NT	5 ♠
◇ A	◇ J 7 4	7 ♠	—
♣ A K Q J 4	♣ 8 6		

You may well wait for a decade for an opportunity to put the convention to work, but as the opening bid of 4 NT is idle in a natural sense and the responses are easy to remember, it is worth while keeping the convention in the bag.

Grand Slam Force

It is convenient to discuss this along with the other commonly-used slam conventions, although it is concerned not with controls, but with trump solidity. Invented by Ely Culbertson, but widely publicised by his wife, the grand slam force is known on the continent of Europe as the "Josephine".

The original convention in its basic form was published in the 1936 Gold Book.

After trump agreement, a bid of 5 NT not preceded by 4 NT is a trump asking bid (TAB). Partner is expected to take the following action:

(1) Holding two of the three top honours in trumps, bid the grand slam.

(2) Lacking two of the three top honours in trumps, bid the small slam.

The convention was slow to catch on, but players eventually realised how effective it could be on hands that contained no losers outside the trump suit. The original version was wasteful of bidding space, however, and extensions soon began to appear. These extensions are many and various, for there are all kinds of holdings the responder may find it useful to indicate apart from two of the three top honours.

My own preference is to keep matters fairly simple in accordance with the following schedule.

In response to the TAB of 5 NT:

> 6 ♣ — shows one of the three top honours.
> 6 ♦ — shows Axxxx or Kxxxx

Six of the agreed trump suit remains the sign-off in all cases. When clubs are trumps there is obviously no room for any extension; one can only confirm or deny the possession of two top honours.

When diamonds are trumps it is possible to indicate the possession of one top honour, which will often be valuable. Holding A K x x x, for instance, partner will be glad to hear that your trumps are headed by the queen.

When a major suit is trumps both extensions can be used. Thus partner, holding A x x x x, can learn about your K x x x x which makes the grand slam a good bet.

By partnership agreement, 6 ♣ can be used as the trump asking bid when 5 NT is not available and when space permits.

Baron Slam Try

This is another method of checking the quality of the trump support. Although it is less precise than the grand slam force and leaves more to the judgement of the responder, it has the advantage of serving small slam as well as grand slam purposes.

The Baron slam try is initiated by a bid at the five or six level in the suit immediately below the agreed trump suit. This asks the responder if his trumps are good in relation to his previous bidding, inviting a jump to six or seven as the case may be.

That is all about slam-bidding conventions for the moment. We shall meet many of them again, and others not yet mentioned, in later pages.

3 · Cue Bidding

A 4 NT convention fills the bill admirably when all you need to know is the number of aces and kings held by your partner, but more subtle methods are required when the object is to locate specific controls. The chosen method of most of the world's players is cue-bidding.

Cue-bidding has been popular with experts even since Sidney Lenz proposed the idea in 1929. Ely Culbertson did not think much of the method, considering it to be imprecise and highly dangerous. There were certainly many nasty accidents involving cue-bids in the early years, for players had yet to learn the lesson that slams were more than a matter of aces and kings. Those were the days when a player would open the bidding on a balanced hand with no more than AK, A (three quick tricks, partner). With a similar holding his partner would make a jump shift, and after agreeing a trump suit the players would cue-bid their aces and kings with cheerful abandon, soaring to the six or seven-level before discovering that the combined hands did not contain the material for a game, let alone a slam.

Players are generally more disciplined nowadays, but it cannot be denied that the proper use of cue-bids calls for a fairly close partnership understanding. The accident risk is bound to be high if you indulge in cue-bidding with an unfamiliar partner.

What is a Cue-Bid?

When a trump suit has been agreed and the partnership is committed to game, there can be no use for the bid of a new suit except as a slam try. All such bids can therefore be regarded as cue-bids, showing a control in the suit (normally the ace or a void) and suggesting the possibility of a slam contract. The first opportunity to make a cue-bid usually arises at the four-level, although it is just possible for a cue-bidding sequence to start at the three-level. Here are some examples.

(1) *W*	*E*	(2) *W*	*E*	(3) *W*	*E*
1 ◇	2 ♠	1 ♡	3 ♡		1 NT 3 ♠
3 ♠	4 ♣	3 ♠		4 ◇	

The last bid in each of the above sequences is a cue-bid. In (1) East cannot wish to play in clubs after spades have been raised. He is showing the ace of clubs and suggesting a slam. In (2) West's second bid commits his side to game in hearts, showing strong values including the ace of spades. In (3) there can be no point in West showing a diamond suit at this stage. Four diamonds is therefore a cue-bid agreeing spades implicitly and showing a hand suitable for slam purposes.

Do not confuse these sequences with others that are similar on the surface.

(4) *W*	*E*	(5) *W*	*E*
1 ♠	2 ♠	1 ♡	2 ◇
3 ◇		3 ◇	3 NT
		4 ◇	4 ♡

In (4) the partnership is not yet committed to game, and West's second bid is a trial bid, not a cue-bid. In (5) East is not cue-bidding in hearts but showing secondary support for his partner's suit, suggesting that ten tricks in hearts may be easier than eleven in diamonds. There is a subtle difference in the following auction.

(6) *W*	*E*
1 ♠	2 ♡
4 ♡	4 ♠

Now East is not suggesting an alternative contract but cue-bidding a spade feature and trying for slam.

Cue-bidding is essentially a co-operative venture, reflecting the philosophy that both partners should play a role in determining the level of the final contract. A cue-bid normally carries the following message: "I have extra strength and control the first round of this suit. What do you think of our slam prospects?"

Thus consulted, the partner of the cue-bidder has several ways of voicing an opinion. With a minimum hand and no slam interest he will simply sign off in the trump suit. If he has extra values and is satisfied about the control position he may go straight to slam. With an in-between hand he may express interest by making a cue-bid of his own. Most players regard this responsive cue-bid, if made below game-level, as showing no extra values but merely indicating a suitable hand for co-operating in a slam venture. A responsive cue-bid that goes beyond game-level, however, is a positive acceptance of the slam try and shows a stronger hand.

A responsive cue-bid will also be the first move by a player who is strong enough to consider the possibility of a grand slam. A series of cue-bids will then identify first-round, second-round and perhaps even third-round controls until it is clear either that the grand slam can be safely bid or that the lack of a vital control makes it necessary to stop at the six-level.

Let us have another look at the hand from page 33 which was found to be unsuitable for Blackwood.

W	E		
1 ♠	2 ♡	♠	K 7
4 ♡	?	♡	K Q J 5 2
		◇	7 6 3
		♣	A 8 3

The knowledge of how many aces West holds will not tell East whether the slam is on or not. He needs information about specific aces, in particular about the ace of diamonds, and the way to obtain it is to make a cue-bid of five clubs.

Note that the first cue-bid is five clubs rather than four spades. In the standard style aces are cue-bid before kings. Let us see how the bidding would proceed on a number of hands that West might hold.

(a) ♠ A Q J 6 4   ♠ K 7   W   E
     ♡ A 9 8 3   ♡ K Q J 5 2   1 ♠   2 ♡
     ◇ 9 5   ◇ 7 6 3   4 ♡   5 ♣
     ♣ K Q   ♣ A 8 3   5 ♡   —

Holding no diamond control West cannot afford to carry the bidding to the six-level by cue-bidding in spades. He signs off in five hearts and East makes a disciplined pass, realising that there must be two diamond losers.

(b) ♠ A Q J 6 4   *W*   *E*
    ♡ A 9 8 3   1 ♠   2 ♡
    ◇ K Q   4 ♡   5 ♣
    ♣ 9 5   6 ♡   —

With firm second-round control of diamonds West goes straight to six hearts, knowing that at worst the slam will depend on a finesse. He would do the same with a singleton diamond.

(c) ♠ A Q J 6 4   *W*   *E*
    ♡ A 9 8 3   1 ♠   2 ♡
    ◇ K 5   4 ♡   5 ♣
    ♣ K 9   5 ♠   6 ♠
                          6 NT —

This is rather more difficult. Holding the kings in both minor suits, West is too good to sign off but is not sure whether six hearts or six no trumps will be the better contract. The cue-bid in spades gives his partner the option, and East's raise to six spades makes it clear that the hand must be played by West. Note that the cue-bid of five spades cannot be construed as a grand slam try, since West denies the ace of diamonds when he by-passes the suit.

(d) ♠ A Q J 6 4   ♠ K 7   *W*   *E*
    ♡ A 9 8 3   ♡ K Q J 5 2 1 ♠   2 ♡
    ◇ A   ◇ 7 6 3   4 ♡   5 ♣
    ♣ 9 5 4   ♣ A 8 3   5 ◇   5 ♠
                          5 NT 7 ♡

At last East hears the responsive cue-bid of five diamonds that he is hoping for. Now he can afford a further cue-bid of five spades, which this time is clearly a grand slam try. When a player has not specifically denied an ace, any cue-bid that commits the partnership to the six-level must be a try for seven. In this case the cue-bid of five spades enables West to take charge by applying the grand slam force, and with two top honours in trumps East bids seven automatically.

The hands will not always fit so well when West has the ace of diamonds, of course.

D

(e) ♠ A 9 8 6 4   *W* *E*
  ♡ A 9 8 3   1 ♠ 2 ♡
  ◇ A K   4 ♡ 5 ♣
  ♣ 9 5   5 ◇ 5 ♠
            6 ◇ 6 ♡

Here all that West can do over five spades is to keep the ball
in play by showing his king of diamonds. From East's point of
view it is significant that his partner has by-passed five no trumps
and six clubs. It looks as though West is worried about the
disposal of a club loser, and East therefore signs off at the six-level.

(f) ♠ Q J 9 8 4 ♠ K 7   *W* *E*
  ♡ A 9 8 3 ♡ K Q J 5 2 1 ♠ 2 ♡
  ◇ A K   ◇ 7 6 3   4 ♡ 5 ♣
  ♣ K 5   ♣ A 8 3   5 ◇ 5 ♠
            6 ♡ —

Since the normal style is to cue-bid the cheapest ace first,
West knows perfectly well that the ace of spades is missing and
is not tempted to explore further.

A different inference may be available when it is the ace of
trumps that is missing.

(g) ♠ A Q J 6 4   *W* *E*
  ♡ 9 8 4 3   1 ♠ 2 ♡
  ◇ A K   4 ♡ 5 ♣
  ♣ K 5   5 ◇ 5 ♠
            6 ♡ —

West knows there is likely to be a hole in the trump suit.
With ♠ K, ♡ A K Q and ♣ A East would not only have forced
originally but would have been able to bid the grand slam himself.

Thus it is seen that the simple cue-bid of five clubs by East
can lead to the correct contract no matter what controls are held
by West. Mind you, it is one thing to construct accurate cue-
bidding sequences on paper and quite another to produce them
at the table under stress. Judgement and discipline are required
from both partners. It is easy to make a false move that may
prove impossible to rectify. Nevertheless, on the majority of slam
hands the use of cue-bidding will result in far greater accuracy
than the blanket application of Blackwood.

Cue-bidding is not imcompatible with the use of Blackwood

or any other 4 NT convention. In fact a cue-bid will often help to steer the 4 NT bid into the right hand—that containing the playing strength.

♠ K Q 6	♠ 8 2	*W*	*E*
♡ 5	♡ A 7 6 3	1 ◇	2 ♣
◇ A K J 8 4	◇ Q 3	4 ♣	4 ♡
♣ K Q 9 4	♣ A J 8 7 2	4 NT	5 ♡
		6 ♣	—

Some players would launch into Blackwood on the second round of bidding. They would land on their feet in this instance, but when clubs are trumps such a move is gambling of the worst kind. West needs to hear some encouraging noise from his partner before he can properly enquire about aces.

Cue-Bidding Secondary Controls

In a normal cue-bidding sequence aces and voids are shown first. It is only when it appears certain that all first-round controls are held that kings and singletons, and subsequently queens and doubletons, are shown. However, there are certain situations in which it is both permissible and desirable for a player to cue-bid a secondary control before all primary controls have been affirmed. The most obvious case is when a player has already denied possession of an ace, as in the Acol sequence 2 ♠—4 ♠. Here is an example.

♠ A Q 10 9 7 6 5	♠ K 8 4 3	*W*	*E*
♡ —	♡ Q 8 6 5	2 ♠	4 ♠
◇ A 10 6 4 3	◇ K 2	5 ♣	5 ◇ (1)
♣ A	♣ J 9 4	5 ♡	5 ♠ (2)
		6 ♣ (3)	6 ◇ (4)
		6 ♡ (5)	7 ♠ (6)

(1) Second-round diamond control.
(2) No more to say for the moment.
(3) Find something more to say.
(4) Well, I have third-round diamond control as well.
(5) Baron grand slam try.
(6) I have it.

The sequence illustrates the intelligent use of cue-bids to identify with certainty all the features needed for a grand slam. It will not always be possible to do this. The limitations of bidding space are such that in many cases there will be no room to discover all we would like to know. Then there is nothing for it but to take a view one way or the other. The optimist will bid the slam and hope that his partner has the right cards, while the pessimist will stay out of it. But the aim of our slam bidding must be to take the guesswork out of these situations, banishing both hope and fear and replacing them by sure knowledge.

A secondary control can often be cue-bid without ambiguity by a player who has limited his hand by giving a negative response to a forcing opening bid.

♠ K Q J 10 5	♠ 7 4 2	W	E
♡ A 7 3	♡ 8	2 ♣	2 ◇
◇ A	◇ 9 6 5 4 3	2 ♠	2 NT
♣ A K Q 2	♣ J 10 8 5	3 ♣	4 ♣
		4 ◇	4 ♡
		6 ♣	—

After the double negative of two diamonds followed by two no trumps it is perfectly safe for East to show his singleton in response to his partner's cue-bid. If he suppresses it the slam will be missed.

Another time when a player may feel impelled to cue-bid a secondary control is when he has a great deal in the way of undisclosed values but no primary control to show.

W	E	♠ A K 10 8 5
1 ♣	1 ♠	♡ 7 2
4 ♠	?	◇ K Q 9 4
		♣ 8 3

With the above holding East is certainly worth a try of some sort, and a cue-bid of five diamonds is a better effort than a Blackwood bid of 4 NT which is always dangerous with a small doubleton in an unbid suit.

It might appear to be treading on equally dangerous ground to cue-bid, in principle promising an ace, when only secondary control is held. A misunderstanding is certainly possible, but East is protected to some extent by the strength of his trump holding which makes it unlikely that West will become over-excited with an unsuitable hand. Here are some possible West hands.

(a) ♠ Q J 7 4	(b) ♠ Q J 7 4	(c) ♠ Q J 7 4
♡ 9 4	♡ A 4	♡ K Q 4
◇ A 7	◇ 8 7	◇ 7
♣ A K Q 9 5	♣ A K Q 9 5	♣ A K J 9 5

On hand (a), holding first-round control of diamonds himself, West will immediately realise what East is up to. Lacking heart control he will have no choice but to sign off in five spades.

On hand (b) West will either go straight to six spades or make a responsive cue-bid in hearts and raise five spades to six.

On hand (c) West may be interested, but he can hardly accept the slam try with only one ace. Again he will sign off in five spades.

Out-of-the-Blue Cue-Bid

This is a term coined by British theorist Norman Squire to describe the bid of a new suit by a player who limited his hand in no trumps on the previous round. The out-of-the-blue cue-bid promises the ace, and implies strong support for partner's last-named suit.

W	E	
		♠ Q 5
1 ♠	1 NT	♡ Q 10 6 3
3 ♡	?	◇ A 8 5
		♣ 9 7 6 3

With such a superb fit East should avoid the lazy raise to four hearts and bid four diamonds instead. Since he cannot possibly wish to play in diamonds, his partner should have no difficulty in interpreting the message. Here is another example.

♠ K 4	W	E
♡ K Q 8 4	1 ◇	1 ♠
◇ A 10 7 6 5	2 NT	3 ♡
♣ A Q	?	

Once again a raise to four hearts would be a poor and un-imaginative effort. A cue-bid of four clubs better indicates the slam potential of the hand.

The out-of-the-blue cue-bid is just a logical extension of the normal method by which a no trump bidder shows good support for his partner's suit.

In the above sequence West's second bid is an indirect or cue-bid raise, agreeing spades as trumps, showing the ace of clubs, and indicating readiness to co-operate if East is slam-minded.

Advance Cue-Bids

The cue-bid by a player who bid no trumps on the previous round agrees his partner's last-named suit by implication. There are other situations, however, in which it is desirable to cue-bid *before* agreeing trumps. Such a bid is termed an advance cue-bid. It may not be recognised as such at the time, but all will become clear to partner when trumps are supported on the next round.

The advance cue-bid is resorted to when a player is too strong in controls to content himself with a raise to game.

East cannot risk allowing the bidding to die at four spades and therefore makes an advance cue-bid in diamonds. From his partner's point of view the trump suit has not yet been settled. On the above sequence East might well be showing a red two-suiter, and West's next move could be to give preference to hearts or even raise the diamonds. But when East supports spades on the next round the meaning of his four diamond bid will be plain.

Choice of Cue-Bids

In the standard style a player starts a cue-bidding sequence by bidding the cheapest of his first-round controls.

	W	E
	1 ♠	3 ♠
	4 ◇	4 ♡
	5 ♣	

Thus in the incomplete sequence above, West's initial cue-bid not only affirms first-round control in diamonds but also denies first-round control in clubs. East's responsive cue-bid promises first-round control in hearts, and West's subsequent cue-bid in clubs indicates second-round control.

At this point, in order to conserve bidding space, East may show a second-round control in diamonds even if he holds the ace of clubs. It is permissible to show controls "out of order" once a player knows that first-round control is held in all the side-suits. Here are the hands and the full bidding sequence.

♠ A K Q 8 3	♠ J 7 6 4	W	E
♡ K Q 5	♡ A 9 6 2	1 ♠	3 ♠
◇ A Q 3 2	◇ 8	4 ◇	4 ♡
♣ 5	♣ A 8 4 3	5 ♣	5 ◇
		5 ♡	6 ♣
		7 ♠	—

It would be wasteful of space for East to bid six clubs over five to show his second ace. By showing his diamond control first he gives his partner valuable information and creates space for West to cue-bid his second-round heart control. When East emerges from the bushes with a bid of six clubs on the next round, West can count thirteen tricks. Note that the cue-bid of six clubs cannot logically be read as indicating second-round control, since East knew at an early stage that his partner lacked first-round control in the suit. Such inferences abound in cue-bidding sequences and must not be missed.

The above is an easy grand slam to bid, of course. Standard cue-bidding methods do not always give such a soft ride. Consider the following example.

♠ A 7	♠ 3	W	E
♡ A 5 4	♡ K 8 6	1 ◇	3 ♣
◇ J 10 9 6 5 2	◇ A K Q 7	3 ◇	4 ◇
♣ K 4	♣ A Q 8 5 3	4 ♡	5 ♣
		5 ♠	?

The bidding has rocketed up to an uncomfortable level without allowing West the opportunity of showing his vital king of clubs. What is East to do? If a bid of five no trumps would be read as a general grand slam try this would give his partner the chance to show his club control, but most players treat the bid of five no trumps as a trump asking bid. East may suspect that his partner, who has made a grand slam try of five spades while missing the top trumps, is likely to have a club control, but he cannot be sure of it. If East shoots the grand slam on this slender evidence he is little better off than if he had used Blackwood on the second round.

To solve the problems caused by this sort of hand, British international player Jeremy Flint suggests that the higher-ranking of touching aces, and the lower-ranking of non-touching aces, should be cue-bid first.

This makes for a more economical auction in many cases. See how easily the Flint cue-bidding style copes with the hand in question.

♠ A 7	♠ 3	W	E
♡ A 5 4	♡ K 8 6	1 ◇	3 ♣
◇ J 10 9 6 5 2	◇ A K Q 7	3 ◇	4 ◇
♣ K 4	♣ A Q 8 5 3	4 ♠	5 ♣
		5 ♡	5 ♠
		6 ♣	7 ◇

The cue-bidding of West's aces in reverse order creates a little extra space at the five-level, enabling East to show his second-round spade control. While not important in itself, this in turn permits West to show his club control at the six-level, after which it is easy for East to bid the grand slam.

The trump suit is excluded, of course, in considering which aces are touching. The easiest way to look at it is to regard all three side-suits as touching in a circle, clubs ranking immediately above spades. In this perspective it is always the higher-ranking of the two aces that is cue-bid first. If hearts are trumps, the first cue-bid is in spades with the aces of spades and diamonds, in clubs with the aces of clubs and spades, and in diamonds with the minor suit aces.

In effect the first cue-bid is always made in the suit immediately below that in which no first-round control is held. The anticipated responsive cue-bid will therefore use up the minimum of bidding space.

When all three aces are held, the first cue-bid is made in the suit immediately below the trump suit.

♠ A 9 4	♠ K 3 2	W	E
♡ K Q 8 7 6	♡ A J 5 2	1 ♡	3 ♡
◇ A K 4 3	◇ 8 5	4 ◇	4 ♡
♣ A	♣ K 7 6 4	4 ♠	5 ♣
		5 ◇	5 ♡
		6 ♣	6 ◇
		7 ♡	—

A valuable inference emerges on the third round. Holding two aces in spades and diamonds, West would have made his first cue-bid in spades. The reversal of the order in the above sequence indicates the possession of all three aces and requires East to show his second-round controls. Later East is able to indicate the third-round diamond control that is essential to the success of the grand slam.

Since this cue-bidding style appears to operate so smoothly, the reader may wonder why it has not been generally adopted. One reason is the fierce resistance to change found amongst tournament players, and another is that the method is by no means perfect. The big weakness of this cue-bidding style is the loss of the happy inference that no first-round control is held in a suit cheaper than that in which the first cue-bid is made.

Thus although the Flint method can be very effective when the initiator of the cue-bidding sequence holds two or three aces, it can lead to difficulty when he has only one.

Consider the following hands.

♠ A Q 2	♠ 7
♡ 6	♡ A Q J 5 2
◇ 10 8 3	◇ A K 5
♣ K Q J 9 7 6	♣ A 10 8 3

For those using standard cue-bidding methods the bidding presents no great difficulty. Here is a normal sequence.

West denies the aces of hearts and diamonds when he cue-bids first in spades. On the next round he is therefore in a position to show his heart control without ambiguity, after which East takes charge.

If Flint cue-bids are used, however, the sequence quickly becomes bogged down.

Over five hearts West can do no more than bid six clubs, and East is left to guess about the vital matters of trump solidity and second-round heart control.

It may be suggested that only the initiator of the cue-bidding sequence should bid the higher-ranking of touching aces, his partner bidding his cheapest ace. That does not solve the problem, however. Even if East bids five diamonds on the third round, West dare not make a bid of five hearts that could be read as ace-showing.

It appears, therefore, that it does not greatly matter which style of cue-bidding is adopted. The gains of each method on the swings will be counterbalanced by losses on the roundabouts. What is important is to have detailed partnership agreement on the method used.

When no Cue-Bid is Available

When control in two side-suits has been confirmed by cue-bidding, a player who wishes to express extra values may find himself with no further control to show. In such cases he can query his partner's holding in the unbid suit by jumping to five in the trump suit.

The message is clearest when the trump suit is a major. Partner is invited to carry on to six if he has second-round control in the unbid suit. Sequences like the following are very common.

		W	E
♠ Q 9 5 4	♠ A K J 8 6 3	1 ♡	2 ♠
♡ A Q J 6 4	♡ K 3 2	3 ♠	4 ◇
◇ 9	◇ A 7	4 ♡	?
♣ K 7 5	♣ Q 4		

East knows that the slam must be a good proposition if his partner has second-round control of clubs, and his bid at this point is a jump to five spades which denies the ability to cue-bid in clubs himself. With his actual hand, West will accept the invitation and bid six. He would do the same if he held a singleton club, but with two or more small clubs he would pass. With the ace of clubs instead of the king, West would bid six clubs to suggest a grand slam.

In sequences of this sort a voluntary raise to five of a major suit has the same meaning as a jump.

		W	E
♠ 5	♠ 9 4	1 ♡	3 ♣
♡ A 10 9 5 4	♡ K Q 7 6 2	3 ◇	3 ♡
◇ Q J 6 4 2	◇ A K	4 ♣	4 ◇
♣ A 3	♣ K Q 9 4	4 ♡	5 ♡
		6 ♡	—

West trusts his partner, bidding six as requested on the strength of his singleton spade.

When the opponents have bid the only suit in which control is lacking, it may be desirable to dispense with cue-bidding altogether.

♠ 7 5			♠ A K Q J 9 8 4 3		
♡ Q 10 9			♡ 5		
◇ A K 7 6 3			◇ 9 4		
♣ A K 5			♣ 10 3		
	W	N	E	S	
	1 ◇	1 ♡	2 ♠	—	
	2 NT	—	4 ♠	—	
	5 ♠	—	6 ♠	—	

In effect the raise to five spades cue-bids both minor suit aces at the same time, telling East that West's only concern is about heart control. This is a much more intelligent effort than a cue-bid of five clubs, over which East might feel bound to sign off in five spades.

When the opponents have not entered the bidding, the bid of five of a major trump suit without checking on controls can have two separate meanings. According to the context it can indicate either (a) all first-round controls held but uncertainty about the texture of the trump suit, or (b) good trumps and general values but no first-round controls to show. The first type of hand is perhaps the more familiar.

♠ Q J 10 6 4 3	♠ 9 8 5 2	W	E
♡ —	♡ K 9 4	2 ♠	4 ♠
◊ A K Q 8 4	◊ 6 2	5 ♠	—
♣ A Q	♣ K J 7 5		

The double raise of the Acol two-bid normally shows two second-round controls but no ace. Here it would be pointless for West to start a cue-bidding sequence, for he is concerned only with the quality of his partner's trumps. The raise to five spades asks the right question. On his actual holding East has no hesitation in passing, but he would have bid the slam if his values had included the king of spades.

Here is another example.

♠ A Q 3	♠ 8 2	W	E
♡ Q J 9 5	♡ K 10 8 6 3	1 ♡	4 ♡
◊ A Q 4	◊ 6 5	5 ♡	6 ♡
♣ A 7 4	♣ K Q 8 3 2		

West scents a slam and queries his partner's trump quality with a raise to five hearts. East carries on to six, deeming it unlikely that there will be two trump losers.

This is the opposite situation.

♠ A 7 6	♠ K Q J 5 3	W	E
♡ A J 10 9 4 2	♡ K Q 6	1 ♡	1 ♠
◊ A Q 10	◊ 9 5	3 ♡	5 ♡
♣ 3	♣ 8 6 5	6 ♡	—

After the jump rebid in hearts East realises that a slam is likely if his partner's controls are good enough. His raise to five hearts gives the message of good trump support, good values in spades, but no control to cue-bid. Holding controls in both minor suits, West has no difficulty in bidding the slam.

♠ K 10 4	♠ Q 2	W	E
♡ K 9 3	♡ A Q J 10 6	2 NT	3 ♡
◇ A K 5	◇ Q J 6 3	4 ♣	5 ♡
♣ A K 8 2	♣ 7 4	6 ♡	—

The message of the five heart bid is "good trumps and a play for six unless the control position is shaky." With adequate controls West accepts the invitation.

The lesson that emerges from this chapter is that cue-bidding, combined with the logical use of the raise to five of a major suit, will solve more slam-bidding problems than all the four no trump conventions put together.

4 · No Trump Sequences

Modern methods of locating a fit, both in major and in minor suits, have done much to disprove the traditional theory about the difficulty of bidding slams after an opening bid in no trumps. Reaching a slam should, in fact, be easier after a no trump opening than after a bid of one of a suit. The no trump opening, normally limited within a range of three points, reduces the problem in many cases to a matter of simple arithmetic. Certainly the responder is well placed to estimate the combined strength and can immediately tell if the hands are in or near the slam zone.

When both hands are balanced a combined count of 34 points is the normal requirement for a small slam. After adding his own points to the minimum guaranteed by the opening no trump bid, the responder should go straight to slam in no trumps if the total comes to 34. It is usually a mistake to look for a trump fit in such cases, for this involves a needless risk. A suit slam is always at the mercy of a bad trump break, and 34 points should produce twelve tricks in no trumps on sheer power.

When the responder knows the combined count to be in the 31-33 point range it is a different matter. A slam in no trumps is unlikely to succeed unless the opener has a maximum, and it becomes advisable to investigate the possibility of playing in a 4-4 trump fit.

The arithmetic changes once again when a long suit is opposite a balanced hand. The power of distribution is such that a slam may now be possible on a combined count of 30, 29 or even fewer points. When so many high cards are missing, however, it becomes necessary to check up on controls. Holding sufficient strength to insist on a slam if the ace-count is right, the responder normally uses the Gerber four club convention.

		W	E
♠ K 9 4	♠ J 6	1 NT	4 ♣
♡ J 6 2	♡ A K Q 8 7 5 4	4 ♠	6 NT
◇ A Q 10 4	◇ K 7		
♣ A J 3	♣ Q 4		

Hearing a 15-17 point no trump opening from his partner, East knows that the combined count may be no more than 30 but does not care. He expects a good play for slam provided that his partner has two aces, and he therefore makes use of Gerber. In this case only a heart lead creates any problem in the play.

Note that the slam must be played by West to give it the best odds. Those who use transfer bids can give themselves an extra chance by playing in six hearts by West, but those who do not must play in no trumps.

Gerber is also used in conjunction with the weak no trump.

		W	E
♠ Q J 6	♠ A K 2	1 NT	4 ♣
♡ K Q 7 4	♡ 3	4 ◇	5 ◇
◇ 9 7 3	◇ K Q J 10 8 5		
♣ K Q 8	♣ A 6 5		

East wisely checks on aces and avoids a hopeless slam.

A Gerber check may be equally advisable after a two no trump opening.

		W	E
♠ A Q J	♠ 9 5	2 NT	4 ♣
♡ K Q 3	♡ 9 6	4 ♠	6 NT
◇ K J 9 4	◇ A Q 2		
♣ A 7 4	♣ K Q J 8 6 5		

From East's point of view slam appears to be a virtual certainty as soon as West opens with a bid of two no trumps. But it is just possible for two aces to be missing, and East checks up before bidding the slam.

The use of Gerber over no trumps frees the immediate raise to four no trumps for service as a quantitative slam invitation. This is useful to the responder on those border-line hands where he needs rather more than just aces from the opener. With a maximum point-count the opener will normally accept the slam invitation. With less than a maximum he should take a closer look at the quality of his points.

In borderline slam decisions the important thing is the presence or absence of controls. Aces and kings are good cards to hold;

queens and knaves less good. A combined count of 30 points is a poor 30 if all four knaves are held since something important is bound to be missing. The opener should therefore consider his controls before accepting or rejecting a quantitative slam try. If his values consist mainly of aces and kings he should accept the invitation even if his point-count is minimal.

Let us look at one or two examples.

♠ A 6	♠ K Q J 8 4 3	*W*	*E*
♡ K Q J	♡ 7 2	2 NT	4 NT
◇ A Q 4 3	◇ K J 5	?	
♣ K Q J 7	♣ 6 5		

East lacks the values to insist on slam, but he is good enough to issue a quantitative invitation. Holding 22 points, West has a maximum two no trump opening. The control position seems reasonably satisfactory, with first-round control in two suits and firm second-round control in the others. West should therefore accept the slam invitation, but it can hardly be sensible to leap to six no trumps and watch the opponents smirk as they cash their two aces. What is the solution?

Having stipulated that the raise to four no trumps is quantitative, I am going to qualify this by suggesting that it is best played as non-forcing Blackwood. The opener is always free to pass, but if he intends to bid on he should do so by showing his aces on the Blackwood schedule. Nothing is lost by such an arrangement and a great deal may be gained. On this understanding, the full sequence on the above hands would be:

W	*E*
2 NT	4 NT
5 ♡	5 NT
—	

Let us look at some other possible two no trump opening bids opposite the same responding hand. Here is one that fits rather better.

♠ A 6	♠ K Q J 8 4 3	*W*	*E*
♡ K 8 3	♡ 7 2	2 NT	4 NT
◇ A Q 4 3	◇ K J 5	6 NT	—
♣ A K 7 2	♣ 6 5		

Although West is minimum in terms of point-count, his magnificent array of controls induces him to accept the invitation. Clearly there is no need for him to show aces in this case.

♠ A 6	♠ K Q J 8 4 3	W	E
♡ Q J 3	♡ 7 2	2 NT	4 NT
◇ A Q 4 3	◇ K J 5	—	
♣ A Q J 2	♣ 6 5		

Here the point-count is again minimum and the control position is not so good. The opener therefore declines the slam invitation.

Non-forcing Blackwood can also be used after an opening bid of one no trump.

♠ K 8 7 4	♠ A Q	W	E
♡ K 6 4	♡ 9 8	1 NT	4 NT
◇ K 10 3	◇ A Q 9 7 6 4 2	5 ◇	6 ◇
♣ A Q 2	♣ 8 3		

Holding good controls, West accepts the slam try by admitting to an ace, and East is happy to raise the fortuitous diamond response.

Mind you, it is too much to hope that you will always be able to avoid bad slams when a long suit faces a balanced hand. In the above example suppose West holds ♠ K 8 7 4, ♡ Q J 4, ◇ K 10 3, ♣ A K J. With a maximum hand such as this he will still respond five diamonds and will find himself playing in slam with two losers in hearts.

But that is not the end of the world. Unless North has both ace and king of hearts there is a good chance that he will not lead the suit. It is certainly better to be missing ace and king in the same suit than to be short of two aces.

Finding a Suit Fit

When the responder does not have a long suit, close investigation may be needed in order to discover a suitable trump suit divided 5-3 or 4-4. In modern bridge the number of ways of doing this is legion. Most players use some form of two club enquiry for major suits in response to an opening bid of one no trump, and many expert pairs use complex and highly specialised methods.

The full Stayman method incorporates the use of two diamonds as a conventional enquiry on minor suit hands and is a complete and integrated system of no trump bidding. An alternative favoured by many players is the Gladiator convention, in which two clubs is a transfer bid used on weak hands, two diamonds enquires for major suits, and two of a major is constructive. Jacoby transfer bids have much to recommend them, since their use creates a number of additional sequences to which special meanings can be assigned. The Blue Club system has its own methods of investigating distribution and point-count after an opening bid of one no trump. With a range of 13-17 it needs them!

Clearly it is neither necessary nor desirable to consider all these methods in detail in a book about slam bidding. In general it will not greatly matter which methods you adopt as long as you are properly organised to discover 5-3 and 4-4 trump holdings in both major and minor suits.

To provide some sort of background for an examination of slam-bidding aids, I shall assume in this chapter that the following simple methods are used.

In response to one no trump:

(1) Two of a suit is weak, except two clubs which is Stayman.
(2) Three of a suit is forcing and indicates at least five cards in the suit.
(3) Two no trumps is natural and invitational.

The forcing response of three in a suit is often the springboard for slam investigation, expecially if it attracts an indirect or cue-bid raise from the opener.

$$W \quad E$$
$$1\ NT \quad 3\ \spadesuit$$
$$4\ \clubsuit$$

As we saw in the last chapter, West's second bid agrees spades as trumps and shows the ace of clubs. This can be a great help when the responder is not quite strong enough to advance beyond game without a little encouragement.

Partners must make sure they are in accord as to the sort of hand that is promised by an indirect raise, for there is no universal agreement on this. Some players hold that it shows really good trumps and a hand suitable in every way for slam purposes, while others take the view that adequate trump support and any outside ace is enough.

No one is likely to quarrel with West's indirect raise on the following hand.

			W	E
♠ K 10 9 4	♠ A Q 8 7 2		1 NT	3 ♠
♡ A 3	♡ K 9 5		4 ♣	4 ◇
◇ J 10 7 4	◇ 2		4 ♡	5 ♡
♣ A J 7	♣ K Q 10 5		6 ♠	—

Although holding only fourteen points opposite a weak no trump, East becomes interested when his partner shows the ace of clubs. He marks time by cue-bidding in diamonds, judging it safe enough to show a second-round control opposite a limited hand. What East really wants to hear is a further cue-bid in hearts from his partner. When this comes he resorts to the Baron slam try and West, whose trumps are as good as can reasonably be expected, bids the slam.

East could hardly have advanced beyond game if West had merely raised to four spades on the second round.

Automatic Aces

This is an alternative way of indicating slam interest after a forcing response of three in a suit. In this method the opener who has a trump fit and a suitable hand for slam purposes is required to show the number of aces he holds by means of a step rebid. The first step (excluding no trumps which denies a fit) shows one ace, the second step two and the third step three aces. A simple raise of responder's suit denies an ace. A similar schedule operates after an opening bid of two no trumps and a response of three in a suit, but now the first step shows two aces, etc.

In some cases it will undoubtedly be helpful to be able to indicate the number of aces below the game level, but the method suffers from the common weakness of bulk ace-showing conventions—it does not specify which aces are held.

If East and West are playing Automatic Aces, the bidding on the previous hand begins as follows:

```
♠ K 10 9 4      ♠ A Q 8 7 2      W    E
♡ A 3           ♡ K 9 5          1 NT  3 ♠
♢ J 10 7 4      ♢ 2              4 ♢   ?
♣ A J 7         ♣ K Q 10 5
```

Now it is quite a gamble for East to advance beyond game. To envisage a good play for slam, East needs to know not just that his partner holds two aces but that they are the aces of clubs and hearts.

Stayman Sequences

When the responder has two or three four-card suits and knows the combined count to be in the range of 31-33 points, he will normally look for a 4-4 trump fit as the safest spot for slam.

Major suit fits are easily discovered via Stayman.

```
♠ K J 6 4       ♠ A Q 8 5        W    E
♡ A 9           ♡ K Q 4 2        1 NT  2 ♣
♢ A J 7 4       ♢ 6              2 ♠   4 NT
♣ Q 3 2         ♣ A J 8 7        5 ♡   6 ♠
```

When the opener bids a major suit after Stayman, the responder's jump to four no trumps is normally treated as conventional. Here East cautiously checks on aces before settling in six spades.

When the opener denies a major suit by rebidding two diamonds, however, the responder's jump to four no trumps is best played as quantitative or non-forcing Blackwood.

```
♠ K Q 8         ♠ A J 6 5        W    E
♡ A 5           ♡ K Q J 7        1 NT  2 ♣
♢ K J 4 3       ♢ Q 6            2 ♢   4 NT
♣ K 10 7 3      ♣ Q J 4          5 ♢   5 NT
```

Having discovered no suit fit, East gives a quantitative raise to four no trumps. With fair controls and a point to spare, West shows his ace but passes quickly when his partner signs off in five no trumps.

The Sharples Convention

When a major suit fit is not brought to light by the use of Stayman, the responder who holds a strong hand may wish to investigate the possibility of a minor suit slam. The normal method, in Britain at any rate, is the four-club and four-diamond convention designed by the brothers Bob and Jim Sharples.

In this method a second-round jump to four clubs by the responder shows a four-card club suit and at least sufficient strength to play in a contract of four no trumps. The opener is expected to raise with four-card support, to bid a new suit at the four-level if he has one, or to sign off in four no trumps.

Here is how it works.

♠ Q J 5	♠ K 7 6 4	W	E
♡ A Q 7 2	♡ 5	1 NT	2 ♣
◇ A 9 8 3	◇ K Q 7 2	2 ♡	4 ♣
♣ Q 7	♣ A K 9 3	4 ◇	6 ◇

The responder has to take his partner's aces for granted in this case, since a bid of four no trumps on the third round would be natural, denying a diamond fit.

Similarly, a second-round jump to four diamonds by the responder shows a four-card diamond suit and denies a club suit. The opener raises with four diamonds, bids a second major suit, or signs off in no trumps.

♠ A 7 5 4	♠ K 8	W	E
♡ K J 7	♡ Q 10 6 3	1 NT	2 ♣
◇ Q J	◇ A K 6 2	2 ♠	4 ◇
♣ K Q 6 4	♣ A 9 5	4 NT	5 NT
		6 NT	—

East's second-round jump to four diamonds shows four cards in the suit (and almost certainly four hearts, since he has denied four cards in either black suit). West can do nothing but sign off in four no trumps, but when East issues a further invitation he bids the slam.

Why jump to the four-level on these hands instead of bidding three clubs or three diamonds? Well, the three-level bids in the minors are required for other purposes. Some play three clubs after Stayman as a sign-off, and three diamonds as Weissberger denoting a major two-suiter with at least five spades. Others use three-level bids in the minors to show five-card or longer suits, offering in the first instance a choice between three no trumps and five in the minor. The point of the Sharples bids of four clubs and four diamonds is that they show specifically four-card suits, which should not be raised with less than four-card support.

After a weak no trump, the responder needs a higher point-count to use the Sharples convention.

		W	E
♠ K 10 3	♠ A 7 6	1 NT	2 ♣
♡ K 9 7	♡ A Q 10 5	2 ◇	4 ♣
◇ Q J 9 5	◇ K 3	4 ◇	4 NT
♣ A 7 2	♣ K Q J 4	5 ◇	6 NT

No fit comes to light, but West treats the natural four no trump rebid as non-forcing Blackwood, showing a little extra strength by admitting to an ace.

After a quantitative raise to four no trumps the opener need feel no compulsion to give a Blackwood response if he has a good reason for doing something else. One good reason is a minimum hand, which dictates a pass. Here is another.

		W	E
♠ A 4 2	♠ K J 6 5	1 NT	2 ♣
♡ K 8 4	♡ A 3	2 ◇	4 ♣
◇ A K J 5 4	◇ 10 8 7	4 ◇	4 NT
♣ Q 7	♣ A K 6 3	6 ◇	—

Realising that there is unlikely to be a shortage of controls in the combined hands, West takes the opportunity to suggest that six diamonds might be better than six no trumps. Holding three-card support, East is happy to agree.

With sufficient strength to go straight to six no trumps, the responder may still use Sharples to investigate grand slam possibilities.

		W	E
♠ K 5	♠ A Q J 7	1 NT	2 ♣
♡ 10 9 4 3	♡ A K	2 ♡	4 ◇
◇ K Q 8 5	◇ A J 6 2	5 ♣	5 ♡
♣ A 8 2	♣ K 7 6	5 ♠	5 NT
		7 ◇	—

West agrees diamonds by cue-bidding his ace of clubs. This is the only indirect raise available in Sharples sequences, since four-level bids are needed to show suits. East is encouraged to make a grand slam try and applies the grand slam force when he hears about the king of spades.

After Two No Trumps

Locating a trump fit after an opening bid of two no trumps is not so easy, because less room is available for exploration. The trouble is that after a conventional enquiry of three clubs the responder's subsequent bids in the minors cannot be restricted to four-card suits. It is therefore desirable to use a method that permits the opener to show his distribution as fully as possible.

In Britain the Baron method of bidding suits up the line after an enquiry of three clubs is popular. A diamond slam is not often missed by those who use this method, but a 4-4 club fit may escape when the opener has a second suit.

A further problem, unconnected with slam bidding, arises when the responder has five spades and four hearts.

W	E	
2 NT	3 ♣	♠ Q 10 5 3 2
3 ◇	3 ♡	♡ K 7 5 4
3 NT	?	◇ 7 6 3
		♣ 9

East does not know whether to pass or bid four spades. Either could be wrong.

Those who bid major suits downwards after three clubs avoid this problem but lose the early opportunity of finding a minor suit fit.

I am going to suggest a complete and precise method of locating a suit fit. It is complex enough to warrant an x-certificate, however, and those who are satisfied with their own methods may prefer to skip the next half-dozen pages.

In response to two no trumps a bid of three hearts or three spades is natural, showing a five-card or longer suit. Three diamonds is Flint (or natural if you prefer it), and three clubs asks for major suits upwards. With no major suit the opener rebids three no trumps on completely balanced hands and three diamonds on all others.

Let us examine the developments after each of the possible rebids by the opener.

3 NT Rebid

2 NT   3 ♣
3 NT

Shows 3-3-4-3 or 3-3-3-4 distribution. If the responder is 5-4 in the majors he can now bid his five-card suit, but he will be less inclined to try for a minor suit fit. Nevertheless:

2 NT   3 ♣
3 NT   4 ♣

Asks opener to raise with four-card support or bid four diamonds.

2 NT   3 ♣
3 NT   4 ♢

Asks opener to raise with four-card support or bid four no trumps.

♠ A K 3	♠ 8 7 6	*W*	*E*
♡ K 7 6	♡ A 5	2 NT	3 ♣
♢ K Q 7 3	♢ A J 5 2	3 NT	4 ♣
♣ A J 9	♣ Q 10 4 2	4 ♢	6 ♢

3 ♢ Rebid

2 NT   3 ♣
3 ♢

Denies a major suit and shows 4-4, 5-4, 5-3 or 5-2 in the minors. The responder can again bid a five-card major, asking the opener to raise with three-card support or sign off in three no trumps. With a minor-oriented hand, however, the responder will be encouraged to explore for marginal slams.

2 NT   3 ♣
3 ♢   4 ♣

Shows four or more clubs.

Opener (*a*) with less than 5 diamonds—raises.

        (*b*) with 4 clubs and 5 diamonds—bids 4 ◇.

        (*c*) with 3 clubs and 5 diamonds—bids 3-card major.

        (*d*) with 2 clubs and 5 diamonds—bids 4 NT.

2 NT	3 ♣
3 ◇	4 ◇

Shows four or more diamonds and denies a club suit.

Opener (*a*) with less than 5 clubs—raises.

        (*b*) with 4 diamonds and 5 clubs—bids 5 ♣.

        (*c*) with 3 diamonds and 5 clubs—bids 3-card major.

        (*d*) with 2 diamonds and 5 clubs—bids 4 NT.

A few examples will indicate the value of obtaining such precise distributional information.

♠ A J 5	♠ 8	*W*	*E*
♡ Q 9	♡ K 10 4	2 NT	3 ♣
◇ A K Q 6 2	◇ J 10 5 4	3 ◇	4 ♣
♣ K Q 6	♣ A 9 8 5 3	4 ♠	6 ◇

The three diamond rebid tells East that a minor suit slam may be a good proposition, and his partner's next bid of four spades tells him which suit to play in.

♠ Q 6 4	♠ K 8 7 3	*W*	*E*
♡ A K 7	♡ 9 2	2 NT	3 ♣
◇ K 4	◇ A Q 7 2	3 ◇	4 ◇
♣ A K J 7 5	♣ Q 8 2	4 NT	6 ♣

As soon as the 5-3 club fit is discovered East knows what to do.

♠ A 9	♠ K 6 5	*W*	*E*
♡ A Q	♡ 8 2	2 NT	3 ♣
◇ A J 7 4 2	◇ K Q 6 3	3 ◇	4 ♣
♣ A J 8 5	♣ K Q 9 4	4 ◇	4 NT
		5 ♣	5 NT
		6 ♣	7 ♣

In the above auction four no trumps is conventional because the club suit has been agreed. If West admits to the king of hearts East intends to play in seven no trumps, but when West denies a king East realises that a spade ruff may be needed for the thirteenth trick.

Players do occasionally open two no trumps with a six-card suit, in which case they will need to cheat with their second rebid. It is important not to lie about the support for partner's suit, however. Four hearts is best reserved as the "cheating" response.

♠ K 5	♠ A 9 4 3	W	E
♡ A 8	♡ Q 6 2	2 NT	3 ♣
◇ A K Q 7 6 4	◇ 2	3 ◇	4 ♣
♣ K 9 4	♣ A 10 8 7 3	4 ♡	6 ♣

West's third bid of four hearts in principle promises a 2-3-5-3 shape. The message is correct as far as club support is concerned, and East is able to place the contract accurately.

Major Suit Rebid

2 NT	3 ♣
3 ♡	3 ♠

Shows a four-card spade suit. Opener raises with four-card support or signs off in no trumps.

♠ J 10 6 3	♠ K Q 9 4	W	E
♡ A Q 7 6	♡ K 2	2 NT	3 ♣
◇ A K 2	◇ 8 6 5	3 ♡	3 ♠
♣ A Q	♣ K 7 6 3	4 ♣	4 NT
		5 ♠	6 ♠

After the cue-bid raise East has only to check up on aces.

2 NT	3 ♣
3 ♡	3 NT

Although it has no relevance to slam bidding, this sequence is included for general interest. The responder clearly has no major suit and is not strong enough to go beyond three no trumps. He should therefore have an unbalanced hand, 5-4 in the minors with a singleton heart or spade. With a semi-balanced 2-3-4-4 or even 2-2-4-5 distribution and a moderate hand, the responder should not bid three clubs but simply raise to three no trumps.

This inference enables the partnership to avoid poor no trump games on hands like the following.

♠ A 3	♠ 8 5 4	*W*	*E*	
♡ A J 7 2	♡ 4	2 NT	3 ♣	
◇ K Q J 4	◇ 10 7 6 3	3 ♡	3 NT	
♣ A J 2	♣ K Q 8 4 3	5 ◇	—	

2 NT	3 ♣
3 ♠	3 NT

The same inference is not available on this sequence, since the responder may have a heart suit. The opener must pass and hope for the best.

When the opener has shown a major suit, the responder may continue the search for a fit at the four-level if he is strong enough to underwrite a contract of four no trumps. The opener's rebids are again used to show distribution.

2 NT	3 ♣
3 ♠	4 ♣

Shows four or more clubs.

Opener (*a*) with 4 or 5 clubs   —raises

        (*b*) with 2 or 3 clubs and 4 or 5 diamonds—bids 4 ◇

        (*c*) with 4-3-3-3 distribution   —bids 4 ♡

        (*d*) with 5-2-3-3 or 5-2-3-3   —bids 4 ♠

        (*e*) with 5-3-3-2   —bids 4 NT

The only rebid that is ambiguous as regards club support is four diamonds. Needing clarification, the responder can bid four hearts. The opener then bids five clubs with three-card support, failing which he signs off in four no trumps.

♠ A K 5 4	♠ Q 7	*W*	*E*
♡ K J	♡ A 5 4 3	2 NT	3 ♣
◇ K Q 7 2	◇ 6 4	3 ♠	4 ♣
♣ A 7 5	♣ K Q 9 6 2	4 ◇	4 ♡
		5 ♣	6 ♣

East counts on a heart ruff for the twelfth trick.

When the opener's first rebid is in hearts he may also have a spade suit, which makes it less easy to define his distribution precisely on the next round.

2 NT	3 ♣
3 ♡	4 ♣

Shows four or more clubs.

Opener (a) with 4 or 5 clubs   —raises
      (b) with 2 or 3 clubs and 4 or 5 diamonds—bids 4 ◇
      (c) with 3-5-2-3 or 2-5-3-3   —bids 4 ♡
      (d) with 3-4-3-3 or 4-4-2-3   —bids 4 ♠
      (e) with 4-4-3-2, 4-5-2-2, 5-4-2-2 or

                                  3-5-3-2—bids 4 NT

After the ambiguous rebid of four diamonds the responder can again use the unbid major—four spades this time—to ask about three-card club support.

If the responder has no more than five clubs he will certainly have a diamond suit as well.

♠ A K 6	♠ 8 7	W	E
♡ K Q 6 3	♡ 5 2	2 NT	3 ♣
◇ K Q 9 4	◇ A 7 6 5 3	3 ♡	4 ♣
♣ A 7	♣ K Q 8 3	4 ◇	5 ◇
		6 ◇	—

East cannot quite bid the slam on his own but, holding a hand suitable in all respects, West goes on to six.

The responder may be single-suited in clubs and yet decide to play in one of his partner's suits.

♠ A K 8 5 4	♠ Q 7 3	W	E
♡ A Q J 3	♡ K 8 7	2 NT	3 ♣
◇ K 8	◇ 3	3 ♡	4 ♣
♣ K 5	♣ A 9 8 6 4 2	4 NT	5 ♡
		5 ♠	6 ♠

After a top-heavy opening bid of two no trumps, the trump suit emerges on the last round of bidding.

There is rather less room for manoeuvre when the responder has no club suit.

2 NT	3 ♣
3 ♠	4 ◇

Shows four or more diamonds and four hearts (with a single-suited diamond hand the responder bids three diamonds on the first round).

Opener (a) with 4 or 5 diamonds   —raises
     (b) with 4-3-3-3 or 4-2-3-4   —bids 4 ♡
     (c) with 5-3-3-2 or 5-2-3-3   —bids 4 ♠
     (d) with 5-3-2-3, 5-2-2-4, 4-3-2-4 or

                    4-2-2-5—bids 4 NT

The opener's rebids on the various sequences may appear complicated at first glance, but they are easy enough to remember if the following points are borne in mind.

1. A raise always shows four-card or better support.
2. A bid in a major suit always promises three cards in the responder's suit.
3. The rebid of a previously-bid major guarantees five cards in the suit, and
4. A bid of four no trumps always shows a doubleton in the responder's suit.

♠ A Q 6 5	♠ 8 3	W	E
♡ A Q 8	♡ K J 10 3	2 NT	3 ♣
◇ A 7	◇ K 9 6 5 2	3 ♠	4 ◇
♣ K Q 5 2	♣ A 6	4 NT	5 NT
		6 ♡	—

When the search for a trump fit seems abortive East issues a quantitative slam invitation. In accepting, West suggests that six hearts may be the best spot after all, and East is happy to go along with the idea.

With a good trump fit and a suitable hand, the opener should not content himself with a single raise.

♠ A 8 5 3	♠ 6	W	E
♡ K Q 2	♡ J 10 8 3	2 NT	3 ♣
◇ A K 6 3	◇ Q 10 7 5 4	3 ♠	4 ◇
♣ A 9	♣ K Q 6	6 ◇	—

Knowing all his cards to be working, West does not make the mistake of leaving the decision to his partner.

This scheme of responses to two no trumps can be equally useful after a two-club opening and a two no trump rebid where the opener shows a balanced hand of 23-24 points.

♠ A K Q 4	♠ 7 6	W	E
♡ A 9 3	♡ 6 2	2 ♣	2 ◇
◇ K 7	◇ A 8 6 4 3	2 NT	3 ♣
♣ A K J 9	♣ Q 10 5 4	3 ♠	4 ♣
		6 ♣	—

Raise to Five No Trumps

A number of players use the raise to five no trumps as a means for the responder to check on minor suits when he has the values for slam in some denomination or other. In a sequence beginning 2 NT-5 NT, for instance, the opener is expected to bid his suits up the line. In similar fashion the raise to four no trumps is used to show a borderline slam hand. If he accepts the invitation, the opener is again expected to bid his suits upwards.

This is a simple and playable method, but those who use the Sharples four-club and four-diamond convention over one no trump and have adequate machinery for exploration over two no trumps do not need the raises to four and five no trumps for this purpose. Four no trumps is released, as we have seen, for use as non-forcing Blackwood, and five no trumps for use as a grand slam try.

The way I like to play it, a bid of five no trumps may have one of five distinct meanings according to the context of the auction. When a trump suit has been agreed, a bid of 5 NT is:

1. The second stage of Blackwood when preceded by 4 NT.
2. A Josephine when not preceded by 4 NT.

When no suit has been agreed a bid of 5 NT is:

3. A sign-off after non-forcing Blackwood.
4. A small slam try when 4 NT is raised to 5 NT. Partner is expected to bid six with a little extra.
5. A grand slam try when it is a jump raise. The hands will be in the 35-37 point range, and partner is expected to choose between six and seven by reference to the quality of his hand.

Here are some examples of the jump raise to 5 NT.

♠ K J 3	♠ A Q 5	W	E
♡ A J	♡ K Q 10 9 2	1 NT	3 ♡
◇ Q J 8 4	◇ A 5 2	3 NT	5 NT
♣ A 8 7 4	♣ K Q	6 NT	—

The opener's hand is in the middle of the 15-17 point range, but his three knaves have a depressant effect. The indications are that something vital is likely to be missing and West settles for the small slam.

♠ A K J	♠ Q 7 2	W	E
♡ A K 3	♡ Q 6	2 ♣	3 ◇
◇ 9 4	◇ A K J 8 3	3 NT	5 NT
♣ A K Q 10 5	♣ 9 8 3	7 NT	—

Holding a super-maximum of 24 points and a near-solid five-card suit, the opener has no hesitation in bidding the grand slam.

5 · Choosing a Trump Suit

A constantly-recurring problem on slam hands concerns the selection of a satisfactory trump suit. The hands on which there is only one reasonable strain in which to play are the exception rather than the rule. On most hands there will be a choice to make—perhaps a straightforward one between a suit and no trumps, perhaps a more complicated one involving as many as four possible denominations. More than any other decision in the area of slam bidding, the exercise of this choice calls for fine judgement.

The difficulty stems in part from the fact that the definition of a satisfactory trump suit changes as soon as it becomes apparent that the hands belong in the slam zone. Any holding of eight trumps in the two hands may be considered an adequate trump suit at the game level, but for slam purposes the requirements are more stringent. Numerical superiority is no longer the only consideration. Equally vital is the question of texture and solidity, for it is self-evident that a loser in the trump suit can be afforded only when there is no loser elsewhere.

Thus, in choosing between two suits of equal length (both divided 5-3, for instance) preference should normally be given to the suit that contains no loser. It may be possible to discard the loser in the other suit on a side winner, but a way of discarding a loser in trumps has yet to be invented.

Mind you, it may not be easy to discover whether there is a hole in the proposed trump suit or not. The grand slam force can do this but only at an uncomfortably high level. Any pair with a method of checking trump solidity at a lower level enjoys a big advantage. We shall be looking at ways of doing this in later chapters, but for the meantime we shall confine ourselves to situations in which trump solidity is self-evident or can reasonably be taken for granted.

♠ K 9 3	♠ A J 10 6 4	W	E
♡ A K 6	♡ 5	1 ◇	1 ♠
◇ K J 9 3	◇ Q 4	2 NT	3 ♣
♣ A 7 2	♣ K Q J 8 6	3 ♠	4 NT
		5 ♡	6 ♣

From East's point of view the spades may or may not be solid. He knows the clubs are solid, however, and therefore bids the slam in clubs in order to take advantage of any extra chances that may be available.

On the above cards six spades is a fair contract which depends on finding the queen. Six no trumps is rather better, for the spade finesse is not needed if the ten of diamonds drops. But six clubs is the best slam of all, giving the declarer a free shot at guessing the position of the diamond ace in addition to the other chances.

Apart from the question of trump solidity, the choice of trumps will often be influenced by the way in which the suits are divided. It is well known that an evenly-divided trump suit often produces an extra trick. This is particularly true at the game level, which accounts for the fact that the early rounds of bidding are so often aimed at locating a 4-4 fit in a major suit.

For slam purposes a certain degree of caution is required. It may still be true that a good 4-4 trump fit, major or minor, will produce an extra trick, but this is likely to happen only on a certain type of hand that is clearly recognisable. In general it is necessary to play in the more evenly distributed trump suit only on the borderline slam hands, containing distributional rather than high-card strength, where tricks have to be made by ruffing.

Here is an example.

♠ Q 8 7	♠ 4	W	E
♡ A Q J 10 3	♡ K 7 2	1 ♡	2 ♣
◇ A K 6 4	◇ Q J 10 5	2 ◇	4 ◇
♣ 3	♣ A J 8 6 5	4 ♡	4 ♠
		6 ◇	—

East's appreciation of his excellent values in support of diamonds paves the way to a good distributional slam. Note that a contract of six hearts would have little chance on a trump lead. Six diamonds is unlikely to fail, however, since the declarer can take his ruffs in either hand.

The advantage of the evenly-divided trump suit stems from a combination of two factors—the facility for ruffing in either hand and the provision of discards on the long suit. A 4-4 trump division may be superior to 6-4 on hands of similar type.

♠ K Q 7 6	♠ A J 9 3	W	E
♡ A J 10 7 4 3	♡ K Q 8 6	1 ♡	2 ♠
◇ Q 5	◇ A 7	4 ♠	5 ◇
♣ 3	♣ J 5 2	6 ♠	—

East forces with the intention of supporting hearts on the second round, but changes his mind when his partner jumps to four spades. This double raise in a forcing situation is used to show good trump support (normally two top honours) in a hand of limited high-card strength. East realises that the hand will play better in spades because his partner's heart suit will provide a parking place for the losing diamond. He therefore cue-bids in diamonds and hits the jackpot when he finds West with a singleton club.

In order to make the correct choice between alternative trump suits with any degree of regularity it is necessary to cultivate the art of visualisation. The player who can form an accurate picture of his partner's distribution during the bidding is in a good position to make a mental prognosis of the course of the play. Considering each potential trump suit in turn, he will thus have a good idea of how many discards will be available and how many ruffs will be needed.

On a distributional hand it will sometimes be advisable to accept a probable trump loser for the sake of the extra flexibility given by the 4-4 fit.

♠ A Q J 8 5	♠ K 7	W	E
♡ 6	♡ A Q 8 5 4 3	1 ♠	2 ♡
◇ K 8 7 2	◇ A 9 5 4	2 ♠	3 ◇
♣ A 9 5	♣ 6	4 ◇	4 ♠
		4 NT	5 ♠
		6 ◇	—

Here the Key-Card Blackwood response of five spades indicates that East holds two aces and the king of spades. West realises that there may not be enough tricks playing in spades, and

therefore bids the slam in diamonds in spite of the strong likeli-
hood of a trump loser.

Six spades is not an impossible contract on the above cards,
but six diamonds is a much better slam, depending on no more
than a 3-2 trump break.

When to Avoid the 4-4 Trump Suit

Danger is a relative matter, and in bidding it is necessary to
balance one risk against another. A trump suit divided 4-4 gives
great flexibility but it is vulnerable against a bad break, tending
to play awkwardly when the outstanding trumps are 4-1, even if
there is no loser in the suit. There is far greater security in a trump
suit divided 5-4, 5-3 or even 6-2, and such a suit should be chosen
whenever it is clear that twelve tricks are likely to be made on
sheer power. In general, when there are plenty of tricks in the
outside suits the slam should be bid either in the longest suit or
in no trumps.

		W	E
♠ 8 2	♠ A K Q 6	1 ◇	2 ♡
♡ K Q 7 3	♡ A 8 6 5	4 ♡	4 NT
◇ Q J 10 5 3	◇ A 8 4 2	5 ◇	6 ◇
♣ A 10	♣ 3		

East bids the slam in the longest suit, reasoning that a potential
heart loser may well be discarded on the spades whereas any
diamond loser is likely to be inescapable. And so it proves. Six
diamonds is practically a laydown, but six hearts requires either
a 3-2 heart break or a winning finesse in diamonds.

A 4-4 fit should be shunned when there appears to be any
possibility of losing two tricks in the suit. There is a great deal of
wisdom in the old maxim—"Do not bid bad suits on good hands."

		W	E
♠ 7 5	♠ A K Q J 3	1 ♡	2 ♠
♡ A J 6 5	♡ 10 7 4 3	2 NT	6 NT
◇ A Q 6 2	◇ K 8		
♣ K Q 7	♣ A J		

When West indicates 15-16 points by rebidding in no trumps,
East is not tempted to support the heart suit. He realises that
twelve tricks are likely to be available on power alone and goes
straight to six no trumps.

♠ A 10 6 2	♠ 9 8 7 3	W	E
♡ K Q J 5 4	♡ A 6 3	1 ♡	2 ◇
◇ A	◇ K Q 9 2	2 ♠	3 ♡
♣ K 7 2	♣ A 8	4 ♡	5 ♣
		6 ♡	—

Not only does East refuse to bid his anaemic spade suit on the first round but he also refuses to support when his partner reverses in the suit. Thus the partnership is never in danger of reaching an unmakeable spade slam.

It is sometimes possible to escape from a dubious 4-4 trump fit even after the suit has been firmly agreed.

♠ K J 4 2	♠ A 10 6 5	W	E
♡ 6	♡ K Q J 7 2	1 ♣	1 ♡
◇ A 8 4	◇ K 5	1 ♠	4 ♠
♣ A K Q J 5	♣ 8 3	6 ♣	—

From West's point of view a small slam appears to be a virtual certainty and the only question concerns the proper denomination. Rather than muddy the waters by using Blackwood, he jumps straight to six clubs. For East the message about solid clubs and doubtful spades is clear. With a suitable hand, East has no hesitation in passing, but with a club less he would convert to six spades or six no trumps.

When there is an abundance of stoppers in the side suits, a contract of six no trumps is likely to be superior to any suit slam.

♠ A J 9 3	♠ K	W	E
♡ Q 6 2	♡ A K 9 5 4	1 ◇	2 ♡
◇ A Q 8 7 5	◇ K 6 3	2 ♠	3 ♣
♣ 7	♣ K Q J 5	3 ♡	4 ◇
		4 ♠	4 NT
		5 ♡	6 NT

Six hearts and six diamonds are both fair contracts, depending on the 68 % chance of an even trump break. But six no trumps is a make when either red suit breaks 3-2, which gives it a 90 % chance of success.

Ruffing in the Short Trump Hand

The choice between suits of equal length can be determined by factors other than general strength and solidity. A slam that is not on in one suit may be possible in another because an extra trick comes from a ruff in the short trump hand. Sometimes this factor will be clearly recognisable in the bidding.

♠ A K Q 9 6	♠ J 10 7	W	E
♡ K Q 3	♡ A J 10 8 4	1 ♠	2 ♡
◇ 5	◇ A 7 6	3 ♣	3 ♠
♣ A 9 8 3	♣ 5 2	4 ♣	4 ◇
		4 NT	5 ♡
		5 NT	6 ♣
		7 ♡	—

When East denies a king West realises that twelve tricks may be the limit in spades or no trumps but that thirteen should be made in hearts by ruffing a diamond in the short trump hand.

The point may be equally valid when both potential trump suits are divided 5-4.

♠ A 4	♠ J 8 3	W	E
♡ A 10 7 6 2	♡ K Q 5 3	1 ♡	3 ♣
◇ A 9	◇ 6	4 ♣	4 ♡
♣ Q 10 5 2	♣ A K J 9 4	4 ♠	4 NT
		5 ♠	7 ♡

Counting a diamond ruff as the thirteenth trick, East bids the grand slam in hearts. Playing in clubs or no trumps East would make no more than twelve tricks.

At times it is desirable to play in the shorter trump suit for the sake of an extra ruffing trick. It can be hard to recognise the virtues of a 4-3 trump fit during the course of the bidding, but the following case is clear enough.

♠ A J 7 5 4	♠ K Q 3	W	E
♡ 2	♡ Q 8 4	1 ♠	3 ♣
◇ A K 9 4	◇ 8 6 3	3 ◇	3 ♠
♣ J 10 6	♣ A K Q 5	4 ♣	4 NT
		5 ♡	6 ♣

When West goes out of his way to indicate a singleton heart, East realises that clubs is likely to be the only denomination in which twelve tricks can be made.

Consideration of Entries

When there is little to choose between two suits in the matter of quality, it is usually best to let the weaker hand become the declarer in order to avoid problems of communication in the play. This can be particularly vital when there is a big difference in the strength of the two hands.

		W	E
♠ A K	♠ 9 6	2 ♣	2 ♡
♡ 7 4	♡ K Q J 10 8 3	3 ♢	4 ♡
♢ A K Q J 6 4	♢ 8 7	6 ♡	—
♣ A K 5	♣ 8 3 2		

East's second-round jump indicates a six-card or longer heart suit containing exactly one loser. This enables West to go straight to the best contract. Six diamonds or six no trumps is defeated if the ace of hearts is held up until the second round.

A broken suit in the weak hand may make a better trump suit than a solid suit in the strong hand.

		W	E
♠ A K Q J 10 5	♠ 2	2 ♣	2 ♢
♡ A 3	♡ K 10 9 7 6 2	2 ♠	3 ♡
♢ A Q 7	♢ 9 4	3 ♠	4 ♡
♣ A K	♣ 8 5 4 3	4 NT	5 ♢
		6 ♡	—

This contract would be most unlucky to go down, whereas six spades and six no trumps are largely dependent on the success of the diamond finesse.

On the next hand it is not easy to pick the one good slam from a group of four candidates.

		W	E
♠ A 10 4	♠ 8 6	1 ♣	1 ♢
♡ A 10 6 3	♡ J 7 5 4	2 ♡	3 ♢
♢ K	♢ A Q J 7 6 2	3 NT	4 ♡
♣ A K Q J 10	♣ 3	6 ♢	—

The key to the success of the auction lies in East's refusal to support hearts on the second round. When East repeats his diamonds and subsequently converts three no trumps to four hearts, the message of good diamonds and poor hearts is unmistakable.

Positional Slams

In earlier chapters we came across one or two example hands on which the choice of denomination was dictated by the need to protect a tenace holding from the opening lead. Experienced players are acutely conscious of this positional factor and allow it to exert a dominant influence on their slam bidding.

Complications sometimes arise owing to a freak of bidding method.

♠ Q 5	♠ A K 6 3	*W*	*E*
♡ 8 6 5	♡ K J 2	3 NT	6 ◇
◇ A K Q 10 7 5 4	◇ 8		
♣ 6	♣ A K Q 7 2		

The ideal contract is six no trumps by East, of course, but once West opens with a gambling three no trump bid East has to bid the slam in his partner's suit in order to protect his king of hearts from the opening lead.

At times it may be advisable to reject a good trump fit on positional grounds.

♠ Q J 7 4	♠ A K 9 8 3	*W*	*E*
♡ K Q J 10 4	♡ 5 2	1 ♡	1 ♠
◇ 2	◇ A K 6 4	3 ♠	4 ◇
♣ A Q 7	♣ 8 2	4 ♠	5 ◇
		6 NT	—

West accepts his partner's second invitation, but bids the slam in no trumps, realising that a club lead might endanger six spades.

6 · Jumping for Joy

Since the forcing takeout requires only a single jump in a new suit, a different meaning can be assigned to a double jump. In the early years of bridge the meaning was generally pre-emptive. Players jumped out of fear rather than joy. The value of pre-emption after partner has opened the bidding has always been open to question, however, and over the years players have come to realise that there are better uses for the double jump response, particularly in the minor suits. The modern tendency is to regard these bids as showing game values with good trump support for partner.

The Swiss Convention

This convention has gained rapidly in popularity since it first appeared some fifteen years ago. After an opening bid of one in a major suit, a response of four in a minor suit is used to show the equivalent of a strong raise to game in the major.

There is certainly a need for some such method in systems like Acol which favour limit raises. Swiss fits in nicely as a substitute for the forcing double raise. Systems incorporating a forcing double raise, such as Standard American, have less need of Swiss, but many players still adopt it for the purpose of showing special features.

There is general agreement on the basic type of hand shown by a Swiss four-club or four-diamond response—big trump support and from eleven to fourteen points. When we probe for further detail we come to a parting of the ways, however, for the Swiss convention has just about as many variations as there are cantons in its land of origin.

It will not be possible to examine all of them here, but we had better have a look at some of the common ones.

1. Ace Swiss

One of the early variations distinguishes between the responses on the basis of ace-content. Four clubs is used to show two aces, four diamonds to show three aces or two aces plus the king of trumps.

After the four-club response, a bid of four diamonds by the opener asks the responder to name any singleton he may hold. Lacking a singleton he signs off in the trump suit. This method soon proved its worth in the bidding of distributional slams on hands like the following.

♠ K 10 8 7 6 3	♠ Q J 5 4	W	E
♡ K Q 6	♡ A 7 4 2	1 ♠	4 ♣
◇ 5	◇ A J 8 2	4 ◇	5 ♣
♣ A 5 3	♣ 6	6 ♠	—

If we alter the responding hand to create a spot of duplication, it is easy to stop at a safe level.

♠ K 10 8 7 6 3	♠ A J 5 4	W	E
♡ K Q 6	♡ 7	1 ♠	4 ♣
◇ 5	◇ A J 8 2	4 ◇	4 ♡
♣ A 5 3	♣ Q 6 4 2	4 ♠	—

The four-diamond response to show three aces or two aces and the king of trumps proved to be a bit of a white elephant, however, and nowadays the four-diamond response is more commonly employed to show two aces but no singleton. The corollary is that the four-club response definitely affirms the presence of a singleton, which in turn means that the responder can indicate a singleton diamond by reverting to the trump suit on the second round.

Although this variation works well on the hands for which it is designed, it leaves us with a problem on strong hands with good trump support but without two aces. The delayed game raise technique of responding two of a minor suit and jumping to four of the major on the next round is not an ideal solution, especially on relatively balanced hands. The next variation aims at including these hands.

2. Unspecific Swiss

The official Acol line, as set out by Terence Reese and Albert Dormer in "Bridge for Tournament Players", is to use the four-club response to indicate a "good" raise to game in the major suit without reference to specific controls or features. The object is simply to distinguish between the distributional raise to game and the raise that is based on high cards.

(a) ♠ Q 10 7 6 3   (b) ♠ K 10 9 4   (c) ♠ Q J 6 4
    ♡ 7 2   ♡ 8 7   ♡ A 9 3
    ◇ K Q 6 5 4   ◇ A 5 3   ◇ A 2
    ♣ 2   ♣ K Q 10 2   ♣ Q 7 5 4

After an opening bid of one spade, the responder raises immediately to four spades on hand (a), but bids a Swiss four clubs on hands (b) and (c).

The four-diamond response is reserved for slightly stronger hands, the sort that merit a slam investigation if the opener holds better than a minimum hand.

(d) ♠ K 10 7 5   (e) ♠ K 4   (f) ♠ 9 5
    ♡ A K 6 5   ♡ A 6 5 4 2   ♡ A Q 9 2
    ◇ K J 7 3   ◇ K J 3   ◇ K 5 4
    ♣ 6   ♣ K 6 3   ♣ A J 6 2

On hand (d) four diamonds is bid in response to an opening bid in either major suit, on hands (e) and (f) in response to an opening bid of one heart.

The Swiss responses are made only on relatively balanced hands, the idea being that any hand with good trump support and a fair five-card suit should use the delayed game raise if not strong enough for an immediate jump shift.

Many Acol players are not entirely happy with this loose style of Swiss, feeling that one of the responses should say something about the ace-content. The whole point of the convention is to enable the opener to judge slam potential below the game level, and half the benefit is lost if the opener cannot tell whether his partner holds an ace or a king-queen combination opposite his singleton.

3. Double-Barrelled Swiss

A further suggestion by Reese and Dormer, stemming from their theory that the immediate jump shift should always show a fair five-card or longer suit, is to extend the use of the Swiss convention to even stronger hands.

With the strength to try for slam opposite a minimum opening bid but with no respectable side suit, the responder starts with four clubs and makes a slam try when the opener signs off.

(a) ♠ A Q		(b) ♠ K 9 4	
♡ K Q 6 2		♡ A Q 7 5	
◇ K J 4		◇ A 5 4 2	
♣ K 7 3 2		♣ A 8	

Playing Double-Barrelled Swiss you respond four clubs to an opening bid of one heart on both hands and make a further try over four hearts, bidding four spades on (a) and five clubs on (b).

This is no doubt a playable method for those who accept the hazard of arriving automatically at the five-level. But many players feel that the bidding space consumed by Swiss can be justified only if the convention is reserved for limited hands in the 11-14 point range. This is the view to which I subscribe. Holding either of the above hands I prefer to make an immediate jump shift in spite of the poor quality of the side suits.

4. Trump Swiss

In this variation the distinction between the responses is made on a different basis. The four-club response emphasises good controls in the outside suits, while the four-diamond response promises good values in the trump suit (at least two of the three top honours).

(a) ♠ Q 9 8 4		(b) ♠ A Q J 4	
♡ 6 2		♡ Q J 6	
◇ A K 8 2		◇ 9 7	
♣ A 9 5		♣ K 8 7 3	

Hand (a) is a typical four-club response to an opening bid of one spade, and hand (b) a typical four-diamond response. When the opener's suit is headed by the ten, it is certainly reassuring for him to hear a four-diamond response.

5. Singleton Swiss

Little known in Britain but gaining in popularity in the United States is a variation in which the responder makes a double jump in his singleton suit. Thus, in response to an opening bid of one spade, four clubs, four diamonds and four hearts all show Swiss-type raises with a singleton in the bid suit. Over an opening bid of one heart, a jump to three spades shows a similar hand with a singleton spade.

Obviously those who adopt this method can no longer use four hearts over one spade, or three spades over one heart, for pre-emptive purposes. But this is no great loss, since there can be little advantage in pre-empting when partner has opened the bidding.

There may be a memory problem in adjusting to the new meaning of these bids, of course. If you open with a bid of one spade and hear a four heart response, instinct and tradition will urge you to pass, but partner will not enjoy being left to play in his singleton suit.

There are clear advantages in announcing the singleton on the first round. The opener is at once in a position to tell whether or not a slam is a likely proposition.

♠ K 6	♠ A 8 5 2	W	E
♡ K Q 9 6 5	♡ A 10 4 2	1 ♡	4 ♣
◇ A 3	◇ K 7 6 5	4 NT	5 ♡
♣ J 8 7 3	♣ 5	6 ♡	—

Good slams can be reached on a minimum point-count when the hands fit well. And when the fit is poor it is easy to stop at the game level.

♠ A Q 7 4 3	♠ K 9 8 6 2	W	E
♡ K Q 10 7	♡ 3	1 ♠	4 ♡
◇ 6	◇ A 8 5	4 ♠	—
♣ Q 6 4	♣ A 5 3 2		

There remains the problem of the responding hands that contain no singleton. In the United States most of the players who have gone over to limit raises have adopted the Kaplan-Sheinwold idea of using the three no trump response as a forcing raise in the major suits. This combines well with Singleton Swiss, the three no trump response showing a strong raise with no singleton.

The Kaplan-Sheinwold school can easily spare the three no trump response for this purpose, since they use a forcing two no trump response to show balanced hands of 13-15 points. Acol players, who use the two no trump response as a non-forcing limit bid, may regard the loss of the three no trump response in its natural sense with a little more concern. But too much concern is out of place. After an opening bid of one in a major suit the response of three no trumps to show a balanced hand of 13-15 points has an elephantine quality that endears it to no one. On this type of hand one can usually get round the problem by responding in a minor suit and taking vigorous action on the next round.

To revert to Singleton Swiss, it should be pointed out that there is a potential hazard in the idea of disclosing the singleton whenever it exists. A defender may be able to double and thus pave the way for a cheap sacrifice without exposing himself to the risk of bidding the suit. Moreover, whether the knowledge of the location of the singleton helps the opener or not, it can do the defenders no harm to be presented with a blueprint of dummy's distribution.

There would appear to be an advantage in reversing the procedure, responding three no trumps when holding any singleton and using the other responses for different purposes. The opener can then take steps to discover the location of the singleton only when he thinks it necessary.

A further point is that none of the Swiss responses so far discussed makes any attempt to disclose a void in the responder's hand. If the identification of singletons is of value in reaching distributional slams, the disclosure of voids must be more so. My own suggestion for a comprehensive schedule of Swiss responses is given below.

6. Super Swiss

If it is accepted that the response of three no trumps and the double jump in the other major suit are not required in a natural sense, we have four different ways of expressing a forcing raise in a major suit.

After a one-heart opening bid, three spades, three no trumps, four clubs and four diamonds are all available as Swiss responses. Similarly, after a one-spade opening bid we have three no trumps, four clubs, four diamonds and four hearts. These responses can be used to progress from the strongest distribution to the weakest, as shown in the following schedule.

Opener   *Responder*

1 ♡   3 ♠ — A void.
          3 NT— A singleton.
          4 ♣ — Two or three aces but no singleton or void.
          4 ◇ — Less than two aces and no singleton or void.
1 ♠   3 NT— A void.
          4 ♣ — A singleton.
          4 ◇ — Two or three aces but no singleton or void.
          4 ♡ — Less than two aces and no singleton or void.

Although a given response has a different meaning according to whether the opening bid is one heart or one spade, there should be no confusion provided that it is borne in mind that the cheapest response shows a void, the next a singleton, and so on.

After a void-showing response, the next step by the opener asks for the location of the void.

♠ A K 4	♠ —	W	E
♡ K Q 7 6 4	♡ J 10 5 2	1 ♡	3 ♠
◇ Q 8 3	◇ A 9 6 5 4	3 NT	4 ♡
♣ K 6	♣ A J 7 2	—	

East reverts to the trump suit to indicate a void in spades and West passes quickly.

♠ K 8 7 6 4 3	♠ A 10 9 2	W	E
♡ A K	♡ 10 8 7 2	1 ♠	3 NT
◇ K 7	◇ A J 5 4 3	4 ♣	4 ♠
♣ Q 4 2	♣ —	4 NT	5 ♡
		7 ♠	—

East's second-round bid of four spades indicates a club void, leaving room for West to check on aces before bidding the grand slam.

Similarly after a singleton-showing response, the next step by the opener asks for the location of the singleton.

♠ Q 9 5 2	♠ 4	W	E
♡ A K J 7 6	♡ Q 10 8 3	1 ♡	3 NT
◇ K Q 3	◇ J 7 5 2	4 ♣	4 ♠
♣ 5	♣ A K J 6	4 NT	5 ◇
		5 ♡	—

West is encouraged when he hears that his partner has a singleton spade, but he subsides at the five-level on learning that two aces are missing.

The only instance in which the opener will be unable to ask for aces after checking on the singleton is when the responder has spade support and a singleton club.

♠ A Q J 5 3	♠ K 8 6 4	W	E
♡ K Q 3	♡ A 6 5 2	1 ♠	4 ♣
◇ 8	◇ A 9 4 2	4 ◇	?
♣ A 9 7	♣ 10		

A return to four spades by East would, as always, show a singleton in the relay suit, diamonds. To show his singleton club East must go to the five-level, which inhibits his partner from checking on aces.

In this one situation, however, it is feasible for the responder to show his aces and his singleton club all together, i.e. four no trumps for no ace, five clubs for one ace, five diamonds for two aces and five hearts for three. Thus the complete auction on the above hands could be:

W	E
1 ♠	4 ♣
4 ◇	5 ◇
6 ♡	7 ♠

West makes use of the Baron slam try to check up on the trump position, and East bids the grand slam on the strength of his king of spades.

On responding hands with no singleton or void, the distinction as to ace-content will be helpful when the opener is on the borderline for making a further move after a Swiss response.

♠ K Q J 6 2	♠ A 9 7 4	W	E
♡ A 7 5 4	♡ K J 3	1 ♠	4 ◇
◇ 2	◇ A 8 7 6	4 ♡	5 ♠
♣ K Q 7	♣ 8 2	6 ♠	—

Knowing his partner to have two aces, West is encouraged to make a further effort and reaches a good slam when he finds his partner with values in hearts.

Give East the king and queen of diamonds instead of the ace and five spades may go down with everything wrong.

♠ K Q J 6 2	♠ A 9 7 4	*W*	*E*
♡ A 7 5 4	♡ K J 3	1 ♠	4 ♡
◇ 2	◇ K Q 7 6	4 ♠	—
♣ K Q 7	♣ 8 2		

West knows immediately that two aces are missing and is not tempted to proceed beyond game.

Note that it is the weakest of our forcing raises—the one showing less than two aces and no singleton or void—that leaves the least room for exploration. That is as it should be. If the opener is strong enough to make a try over this response there can be little danger for him in a venture to the five level.

Those who feel strongly on the matter can dispense with the distinction regarding ace-content and use the two weaker Swiss responses as Trump Swiss.

7. Minor Suit Swiss

This is another bright idea from Terence Reese and Albert Dormer, who point out that hands strong in support for partner's minor suit can be hard to express without going beyond three no trumps.

When partner opens one club, the following hands are certainly awkward for those who use limit raises.

(*a*) ♠ A Q 3	(*b*) ♠ K 5	(*c*) ♠ 6 5 4 2
♡ 6 3	♡ 7 6 3	♡ Q 7
◇ 8 6 4	◇ A J 3	◇ K Q 5
♣ A K J 7 4	♣ K Q 8 5 2	♣ A Q 8 3

A non-forcing raise to three clubs is out of the question on such hands, yet there is no reasonable side-suit to bid. The suggestion is that double jumps to three hearts and three diamonds be used to indicate strong and less strong Swiss raises. Here hand (*a*) qualifies for a three heart response, hands (*b*) and (*c*) for three diamonds.

Similarly in response to one diamond, jumps to three spades and three hearts are Swiss raises in descending strength.

(d) ♠ Q J 5	(e) ♠ 8 7	(f) ♠ A 5
♡ 7 2	♡ K Q 4	♡ 7 5 4 2
◇ A K Q 5	◇ K Q 8 7 5	◇ K 10 9 6 5
♣ J 5 4 2	♣ K 3 2	♣ A Q

Hands (d) and (e) rate a three heart response while hand (f) qualifies for three spades.

Minor suit Swiss is best treated as forcing only to four of the minor. Eleven tricks may be beyond reach if the opener has a minimum hand.

An alternative treatment which I recommend is to abandon the distinction as to strength and jump in the suit in which a secure stopper is held, thus helping partner to judge if three no trumps is on. On this basis hands (a), (d) and (f) would respond three spades, hand (b) and (c) three diamonds and hands (e) three hearts.

That leaves us without a suitable response to an opening bid of one diamond on a hand like the following.

$$\spadesuit\ 8\ 3$$
$$\heartsuit\ 7\ 6\ 3$$
$$\diamondsuit\ A\ K\ 8\ 5\ 4$$
$$\clubsuit\ A\ Q\ 6$$

Still, we are no worse off than at present. We can always respond two clubs and hope to be able to judge matters on the next round.

Intervention

It is possible to play all forms of Swiss after a takeout double by the enemy, although the situation is not likely to arise very often. After an enemy overcall, however, it is better to revert to natural bidding. The cue-bid in the opponent's suit is available to express a strong raise.

8. Reverse Swiss

A number of players favour Swiss raises by the opener after a response of one or two in a suit.

G

♠ A Q 5 2	♠ K 9 8 6 3	W	E
♡ A 7	♡ K 8 4	1 ◇	1 ♠
◇ K Q J 5 4	◇ A 3	4 ♣	4 ◇
♣ K 9	♣ 7 6 4	4 ♡	5 ♠
		6 NT	

This is Reverse Swiss in action. The opener's second bid of four clubs indicates a high-card, as opposed to a distributional, raise to four spades. Cue-bids in diamonds and hearts follow, and when East shows extra values by jumping to five spades West bids the slam in no trumps in order to protect his king of clubs.

A Swiss raise on the second round does not always have to involve a double jump.

♠ A K 5 3 2	♠ Q 6	W	E
♡ A Q 6 2	♡ K J 10 5 4	1 ♠	2 ♡
◇ 8 3	◇ K 9 2	4 ♣	4 ♡
♣ A K	♣ 8 6 4	4 ♠	5 ◇
		6 ♡	—

A rebid of three clubs by West would have been unconditionally forcing, hence the single jump to four clubs is available as Swiss.

In such sequences there seems little point in ascribing different meanings to the bids of four clubs and four diamonds. The distinction between a high-card raise and one based on distribution should be enough.

By partnership agreement Swiss can be used by the responder on the second round.

♠ A K 5 4	♠ Q 10 7 2	W	E
♡ K 7	♡ A Q J 4 2	1 ♣	1 ♡
◇ 10 4	◇ A 8 5	1 ♠	4 ◇
♣ A 9 6 4 3	♣ 5	4 ♡	5 ◇
		6 ♠	—

Knowing his partner to be heavy in top cards, West makes an effort with four hearts and bids the slam when East cue-bids in diamonds.

♠ K Q 9 6 5	♠ 3	W	E
♡ Q J 8 7 2	♡ A K 5 3	1 ♠	2 ◇
◇ A 5	◇ K 9 7 4 2	2 ♡	4 ♣
♣ 6	♣ A 7 4	4 ◇	4 NT
		5 ◇	6 ♡

These second-round Swiss bids have something in common with the jumps used in the Blue Club system to show a superfit. The difference is that in Blue Club the responder indicates precise controls in his suits when he jumps in this manner.

I used Swiss on the second round for several years and found that it worked well enough when the right hands came along. There are other methods of dealing with such hands, however, and I eventually came to the conclusion that second-round jumps should be made to serve a more precise purpose.

Fragment Bids

Originated by Monroe Ingberman of Chicago, this idea has caught on in the United States but has not gained much support in Britain. The double jump in a new suit on the second round of bidding is used to show big trump support, a "fragment" of two or three cards including a high honour in the bid suit, and a shortage (singleton or void) in the fourth suit.

Like second-round Swiss the fragment bid amounts to a high-card raise to game of partner's major suit, but it does give more specific information. The knowledge of the presence and the location of a singleton is always a great help in the bidding of slams based on distribution.

♠ A Q 6	♠ K 7	W	E
♡ K 8 7 3	♡ Q J 9 5 2	1 ♣	1 ♡
◇ 5	◇ A 7 6 4	3 ♠	4 NT
♣ A K 8 5 4	♣ 7 3	5 ♡	6 ♡

The slam is not hard to reach after West's fragment bid of three spades on the second round.

Some players prefer to use Splinter Bids, whereby the jump is made in the singleton rather than in the fragment suit. There is not much difference. The Splinter Bid auction on the above hand would take a similar course.

W	*E*
1 ♣	1 ♡
4 ◇	4 NT
5 ♡	6 ♡

Again the slam is reached without difficulty.

Either Fragment or Splinter Bids can be used equally well by the responder.

♠ A J 7 5	♠ K Q 8 2	*W*	*E*
♡ A 3	♡ K J 7 6 2	1 ◇	1 ♡
◇ Q 9 6 4 3	◇ 7	1 ♠	4 ♣
♣ K 5	♣ A 9 2	4 ♡	4 NT
		5 ♡	6 ♠

Fragment-type bids can also be used by the responder when the opener rebids his major suit.

♠ K 8	♠ A J 6 4 3	*W*	*E*
♡ A Q 10 7 3	♡ K 9 2	1 ♡	1 ♠
◇ 8 6 5	◇ 4	2 ♡	4 ♣
♣ A 9 4	♣ K Q 6 2	4 NT	5 ◇
		6 ♡	—

The knowledge that his partner has a singleton diamond makes it easy for West to envisage the slam.

Once it is accepted that this type of jump guarantees a singleton in the fourth suit, a valuable inference emerges when the responder fails to jump on the second round.

♠ K 8	♠ A J 6 4	*W*	*E*
♡ A Q 10 7 3	♡ K 9 2	1 ♡	1 ♠
◇ 8 6 5	◇ 4 3	2 ♡	3 ♣
♣ A 9 4	♣ K Q 6 2	3 ♠	4 ♡
		—	

West knows that his partner cannot have a singleton diamond since he did not jump to four clubs at his second turn. West is therefore not tempted to proceed beyond game.

Although there is a great deal to be said for Fragment Bids, I believe that there is a still better way of harnessing second-round and later jumps.

Void-Showing Jumps

Having been working towards this idea from the beginning of the chapter, I am a little surprised that it has taken so long to arrive.

Hands containing good trump support and a void may not turn up so very often, but they present a real problem when they do. The slam potential of such hands is enormous, yet it can be hard to find the bidding space to express all the features accurately. It is for this reason that I believe that double jumps on the second round are best reserved for this type of hand.

This is not a new idea by any means. Ely Culbertson suggested a void-showing bid at one time in the distant past, and in Britain as in other countries a number of expert pairs have been using something of this nature with great success for the past twenty-five years or more.

Here is how the bid works.

♠ 7 4 2	♠ A 5	W	E
♡ A Q 6 4	♡ K 9 8 3 2	1 ◇	1 ♡
◇ A K Q 10 7 3	◇ 8 4	4 ♣	4 ♠
♣ —	♣ J 9 6 2	5 NT	6 ◇
		7 ♡	—

The knowledge that West is void in clubs encourages East to venture beyond the game level in spite of his minimal values. All that remains for West to do is to apply the grand slam force.

A double jump is not always required to put across the message of a void with good trump support. A single jump is sufficient whenever the bid of the suit without a jump would be forcing.

♠ —	♠ J 10 7 6	W	E
♡ A K 7 6 4 3	♡ Q J 8 5	1 ♡	3 ♡
◇ A 8 5 4	◇ 6	4 ♠	4 NT
♣ A 6 5	♣ K Q 8 2	5 ♠	6 ◇
		7 ♡	—

The great advantage of showing a void is that it enables partner to judge whether his high cards are working or not. No doubt this grand slam can be bid by other methods, but the void-showing leap makes for a short, sweet auction.

When a void has been indicated in this manner, the ace of the suit must be suppressed in response to a subsequent four no trump enquiry.

♠ K Q 6 2	♠ A 10 9 7 4	W	E
♡ K Q 9 7 5 4	♡ A 3	1 ♡	1 ♠
◇ —	◇ A Q 6 5	4 ◇	4 ♡
♣ K Q 7	♣ 8 5	4 NT	5 ♡
		6 ♠	—

When West shows good spade support and a diamond void, East marks time with a cue-bid in hearts, giving his partner the chance to introduce Blackwood. Since the ace of diamonds is known to be a non-working ace, East tucks it behind the queen and responds as though he had only two aces. This enables West to place the contract at the right level.

Had East held the ace of clubs instead of the ace of diamonds his response would have been five spades, and West would have bid the grand slam with confidence.

In the final of the 1971 Bermuda Bowl contest at Taipei, a French pair bid Board 62 as shown below.

♠ A Q 10 4 3	♠ K J 7 6 2	W	E
♡ —	♡ A 8 7		1 ♠
◇ K 10 9 6 5 4	◇ A Q	2 ◇	2 ♠
♣ 7 4	♣ J 6 5	4 ♠	—

That turned out all right in practice since the opponents had two club winners to cash. But if East's heart and club holdings had been reversed a cold grand slam would have been missed.

Playing void-showing jumps West bids four hearts on the second round. East is then able to make an informed decision instead of fumbling in the dark.

The next hand was bid by Nico Gardener and the late Albert Rose during a British tour of South Africa in 1962.

♠ 7 6	♠ A 9	W	N	E	S
♡ —	♡ 10 6 5	Rose		Gardener	
◇ A 8 6 5 4 2	◇ K Q 7	1 ◇	1 ♠	3 ♣	—
♣ K Q 9 7 4	♣ A J 8 5 2	4 ♡	—	4 ♠	—
		5 ♣	—	7 ♣ all pass	

East's hand became enormous when West disclosed good club support and a void in hearts. Although West refused to cue-bid his ace of diamonds on the next round, East was not taking much of a risk when he bid the grand slam.

A jump in the enemy suit carries the same conventional message of a void in the suit along with excellent trump support. This is the one occasion when a void can be shown on the first round of bidding.

♠ A K 8 7 3	♠ Q J 6 4	W	N	E	S
♡ K J 5	♡ Q 10 8 2	1 ♠	2 ◇	4 ◇	—
◇ K 9 4 3	◇ —	4 NT	—	5 ◇	—
♣ 7	♣ A K J 5 2	6 ♠	all pass		

The void-showing leap may appear to be wasteful of bidding space, but in fact it simplifies partner's problems to such an extent that bidding space is saved in the long run.

Having specified that the double jump shows a void, I now propose to qualify this by admitting that a singleton ace will do as well. Even a doubleton ace-king holding need not be ruled out. The message of the double jump is thus modified to read, "Good trump support and probably a void but certainly no losers in this suit." Provided that the player who makes the jump remembers that he must not show the ace a second time in response to Blackwood he is not likely to come to any harm.

The three examples that follow are all taken from the Bidding Challenge feature in Bridge Magazine.

♠ 10 8 2	♠ A	W	E
♡ K 3	♡ 8 6		1 ◇
◇ K 5 2	◇ A Q 10 7 4	2 ♣	3 ♠
♣ K 10 8 3 2	♣ A Q 9 6 4	4 NT	5 ♡
		6 ♣	—

Since most players regard a reverse after a two-level response as forcing, the single jump to three spades denotes no losers in the suit. In response to four no trumps East suppresses the ace of spades and West places the contract accurately. It is, of course, fortuitous that the slam is played from the right hand.

♠ A Q 10 8 7	♠ K 9 6 2	W	E
♡ 10 6 4 3	♡ A J 7		1 ♣
◇ 6	◇ A K	1 ♠	4 ◇
♣ Q J 4	♣ A 8 7 3	4 ♠	—

The reverse after a one-level response is not forcing in the Acol system, and East has to make a double jump to show spade support and no diamond losers. West is immediately warned of the duplication in diamonds and is not tempted to venture to an unsafe level. West would have been interested had his heart and diamond holdings been reversed, however.

♠ J 9 8 4	♠ A	W	E
♡ A Q 10 7 5	♡ —	1 ♡	3 ♣
◇ —	◇ K Q 3 2	4 ◇	5 ♠
♣ A 10 9 3	♣ K Q 8 7 6 5 4 2	5 NT	7 ♣

It is not often that there is room for both players to make a control-showing jump. In this case East might almost have bid the grand slam on the second round.

Since we are admitting singleton aces and doubleton ace-kings to the party, we had better stop talking about void-showing jumps. In future we shall refer to all such leaps, whether they show a void or an ace, as jump cue-bids.

At the risk of being repetitive I should like to set out definitively the requirements for a jump cue-bid.

1. Game values.
2. Good four-card or better support for the last-named suit (unless trumps have been agreed specifically).
3. No losers in the bid suit.

Here is a hand from the 1970 European Championships at Estoril where a jump cue-bid in the opponent's suit could profitably have been employed. In the match against France a British pair bid as follows:

♠ A J 6 5 3	♠ K Q 9 4	W	N	E	S
♡ A	♡ J 10 8 3			1 ♠	2 ♡
◇ Q J	◇ K 8 4	3 ♣	—	3 NT	—
♣ Q J 7 4 2	♣ A K	4 ♠	all pass		

Although West had in theory shown the values for a delayed game raise, East did not consider it altogether safe to make another move.

The use of the jump cue-bid makes the bidding very simple.

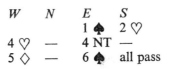

The slam was also missed by France in the other room, which proves once again that slam bidding is much easier on paper than it is at the bridge table.

Having cleared the decks of some subsidiary detail, we are now ready to tackle Byzantine.

7 · Byzantine Four No Trumps

The most modern and dynamic of all the four no trump conventions is a product of the fertile brain of J. C. H. Marx, who has already contributed so much to bidding theory. Jack Marx is the surviving member of the famous quartet that included S. J. Simon, M. Harrison Gray and Iain Macleod. In the mid-thirties these four hammered out the basic structure of the Acol system and went on to win every tournament in sight.

As well as playing a major role in designing the Acol system, Marx was a pioneer of the conventional use of two clubs in response to an opening bid of one no trump as a request for major suits. With better publicity at the time the convention might today have been known as Marx instead of Stayman.

Known to British experts of my generation as "The Headmaster" and to the younger and less reverent as "Big Daddy Acol", Jack Marx is a veteran member of the Selection Committee of the British Bridge League. One of the highlights of his long and distinguished playing career came in 1950 when he was a member of the winning British team in the European Championships. And as recently as 1971 he showed that he had lost none of his skill when he again put his name on Britain's premier trophy, the Gold Cup, thirty-four years after his first success in the event.

But I believe that Marx may yet become best known as the originator of Byzantine. When this convention is more widely known it will be recognised as marking a revolutionary advance in slam-bidding technique. It is not a suitable tool for casual players, but for regular partners determined to make a mark in the tough world of tournament bridge it is the most valuable weapon ever designed.

The germ of the idea was planted in the mind of Marx in the early sixties, when Roman Blackwood first came to the attention of players in this country. This accounts for the choice of name, by analogy with the development of the Byzantine Empire from the Roman.

At that time Marx, in common with a number of top British players, was still an exponent of the Culbertson 4-5 which was the official slam convention of the Acol system. In the United States and elsewhere the convention was all but defunct, but in Britain it lingered on, due in no small measure to the vigorous advocacy of the late S. J. Simon, who in his books had described it as an adult weapon compared with the child's toy of Blackwood.

However, there could be no doubt that the Culbertson 4-5 was losing ground even in Britain. More and more players, experts included, were drifting away towards Blackwood, taking the view that the push-button simplicity of the method made up for any lost efficiency.

Thus Marx was in the frame of mind to look for a replacement, although reluctant to abandon the idea of the "bid" king that was the basis of the effectiveness of the Culbertson method. The dual function of the five-club and five-diamond responses in Roman Blackwood had an obvious appeal, but the uses to which the remaining responses of five hearts, five spades and five no trumps were put seemed wasteful and almost trivial. It occurred to Marx that more mileage might be obtained from the convention if the king of a bid suit could be substituted for an ace in some of the responses. And if one bid king could be substituted why not all bid kings? What about bid queens? It seemed highly desirable to pack as much information as possible into the first response to four no trumps, thus leaving fewer extra features to be shown on the next round. The question of how far it was safe to go in this first response without creating ambiguity about the number of primary controls held could be decided only by experiment.

These ideas gradually took form, but it was not until 1965, when Marx was convalescing after a serious illness, that he found the time to give his complete attention to Byzantine. He was sleeping badly at night, and as an alternative to barbiturates took to dealing out bridge hands for an hour or so before going to bed. A promising hand of thirteen cards would be selected and the remaining thirty-nine cards dealt at random to form three supporting hands. Pursued over the course of three or four months, this practice was a therapeutic success and led to certain firm conclusions.

1. It was unsafe to include all bid kings in the responses.
2. Kings included should belong to one of two carefully defined categories—"key" kings and "half-key" kings.
3. Kings substituted for aces should not exceed one.
4. "Key" queens could be shown only if attached to kings.
5. There should be no more than two "key" suits.

Having put the convention down on paper in a rough and ready form, Marx persuaded the brothers Bob and Jim Sharples, who have the reputation of being the most successful slam bidders in the country, to act as guinea pigs. The result was instant success and a full licence for the convention was soon obtained. Since that time Byzantine has been well tested by a number of early converts, including the Sharples twins, Joe Amsbury, Carl Hille, Marius Wlodarczyk, and latterly Tom Culbertson and myself. That only a few trifling changes have been found necessary since the introduction of the convention is testimony to the thoroughness with which Marx did his spade-work.

Before setting out details of the responses it is necessary to define our terms.

Key Suit

1. When there is only one key suit this is the trump suit, whether agreed specifically or implicitly. Implicit agreement can take several different forms, apart from the indirect raise and the jump cue-bid.

(a)   W   E
             1 ♡   3 ♣
             3 ◇   4 NT

In most auctions a jump to four no trumps implies support for partner's last-named suit. In the above example East is agreeing diamonds as trumps, since with heart support he could have agreed the suit specifically below the game level.

(b)   W   E
             1 ♡   3 ◇
             3 ♠   4 NT

When there is no space to agree the first suit below the level of game, the first suit is implicitly agreed by a bid of four no trumps.

This will happen only when the auction contains elements of both force and reverse. In the above case East agrees hearts, not spades.

(c) W   E
1 ♡ 2 ♠
3 ◇ 3 ♠
4 ◇ 4 NT

When the responder has forced and repeated his suit, his subsequent four no trump bid denies interest in either of his partner's suits. In the above sequence spades is the only key suit.

2. A second key suit may be either (a) any genuine suit bid and supported.

W   E
1 ♠ 3 ◇   Here spades and diamonds
4 ◇ 4 ♠   are both key suits.
4 NT

Or (b) any suit in response to no trumps when the no trump bidder has not previously bid a suit.

W   E
1 NT 3 ♡   Hearts and diamonds are
3 ♠ 4 ◇   both key suits.
4 ♡ 4 NT

W   E
1 ◇ 3 NT   Diamonds and clubs are
4 ♣ 4 ◇   both key suits.
4 NT

Key kings and king-queens, designated K and KQ in the table overleaf, are shown in certain Byzantine responses.

Half-Key Suit

This is a genuine suit bid by one partner but not supported. Suits in which artificial bids such as Stayman, fourth-suit forces and cue-bids are made are excluded.

When there is only one key suit, half-key kings, designated (K) in the table overleaf, are shown in certain Byzantine responses.

If a side suit has been mentioned by the 4 NT bidder, a (K)

included in the response must belong to that suit and not to one bid by his partner. If the 4 NT bidder has bid no suit other than trumps, his partner can show a (K) in his own suit.

Now for the responses. I shall first set these out in tabular form and then go on to discuss each response in some detail.

BYZANTINE RESPONSES TO 4 NT

	With One Key Suit	*With Two Key Suits*
5 ♣ —	0 or 3 aces or AA*K*	0 or 3 aces or AA*K*
5 ◇ —	1 or 4 aces or AAA*K*	1 or 4 aces or AAA*K*
5 ♡ —	2 aces or A*KQ* or A*K*(K)	2 aces or A*KQ* or A*KK*
5 ♠ —	AA*KQ* or AAA(K)	AA*KQ* or AA*KK* or A*KQK*
5 NT—	AAA*KQ* or AAAA*K* or AA(K)	AAA*KQ* or AAA*KK* or AAAA*K* or AA*KQK* or A*KQKQ*

Do not allow yourself to be put off if the table appears complex at first glance. A little practice will soon make everything clear.

When to Bid 4 NT

Either partner may start the machinery when he is satisfied that the values for slam may be present. No hard and fast rules are laid down, but a bid of 4 NT does imply a measure of control in the side suits. With a small doubleton in an unbid suit a different slam try should be chosen.

In general it is preferable for the hand that is weaker in controls to start the proceedings, but the versatility of the convention is such that on many hands either partner can bid 4 NT with satisfactory results.

When the agreed suit is a minor, the usual care is required in checking that the response cannot carry the bidding too high. The Blackwood procedure for stopping at 5 NT via the bid of a new suit at the five-level is not available.

5 ♣ Response

This is the response for all ace-less hands regardless of the other cards held. As in Roman Blackwood this response is also used to show three aces, with the difference that a key king may be substituted for one of the aces.

One advantage of Byzantine is that the first response will very often tell the whole story, making further investigation unnecessary.

♠ A Q J 9 4	♠ K 3	W	E
♡ A 6	♡ K Q 10 8	1 ♠	2 ◇
◇ A 8 7 4 3	◇ Q 10 6 5 2	4 ◇	4 NT
♣ 7	♣ A 9	5 ♣	6 ◇

The 5 ♣ response indicates at once that either an ace or the king of trumps is missing, and East can place the contract without delay.

There will normally be no difficulty in working out whether a 5 ♣ response shows three aces or none. If the 4 NT bidder has only one ace he is likely to be loaded with kings and queens and will know from the bidding that his partner cannot be ace-less.

Ambiguity will occasionally rear its head when the 4 NT bidder has two aces, however. He may not always be able to tell whether the 5 ♣ response indicates no ace or two aces and the king of trumps. When in doubt it is his duty to sign off at the five-level. A partner whose previous bidding is not inconsistent with an ace-less hand will naturally continue when he holds two aces and the king of trumps.

♠ 7 4	♠ A K Q J 5	W	E
♡ A K 9 3	♡ Q J 10 4 2	1 ◇	2 ♠
◇ A J 10 6 4	◇ 8	3 ♡	4 NT
♣ J 3	♣ A 5	5 ♣	5 ♡
		6 ♡	7 ♡

East signs off in five hearts in order to avoid a calamity when his partner has no ace. West clarifies the position by raising to six, after which East can count thirteen tricks.

The position is a little more awkward when the agreed trump suit is clubs. The solution is for the partner of the 4 NT bidder, holding AA*K*, to regard his *K* as a (K) and respond 5 NT instead of 5 ♣.

♠ A K 9 8 4	♠ Q 5	W	E
♡ K Q 6	♡ 2	1 ♠	2 ♣
◇ 6	◇ K Q J 8	4 ♣	4 ◇
♣ A Q 8 3	♣ K J 9 7 6 2	4 NT	5 ♣

After the jump to four clubs East feels he is worth an effort, although he clearly cannot afford to bid 4 NT himself. He therefore cue-bids a second-round control, but signs off in 5 ♣ over 4 NT. West must trust his partner and pass, for with two aces and the king of clubs East would have chosen the 5 NT response.

5 ◇ Response

This shows one ace or four, and in the latter case it is again permissible to substitute a key king for an ace.

The Roman 2 ◇ auction below shows how skilled players can manipulate the early bidding so as to obtain required information. The hand was bid by the Sharples brothers in the final of the Four Star team event at Brighton a few years ago.

♠ —	♠ A K Q J 10 8 4 3	W	E
♡ A J 9 3	♡ 6	2 ◇	2 NT(1)
◇ A Q 10 6 4	◇ 7	3 ♠(2)	4 ♣(3)
♣ A K 6 2	♣ Q 7 5	4 ◇(4)	4 NT(5)
		5 ◇	7 NT

(1) Positive response.
(2) Shortage.
(3) Natural. The trump suit as far as West is concerned.
(4) Five-card suit.
(5) Confirming clubs as trumps!

The Byzantine 5 ◇ response, showing three aces and the king of clubs, was just what East wanted to hear.

Ambiguity will arise very infrequently with the 5 ◇ response. In the tricky situation where the agreed trump suit is diamonds the problem can be overcome by making a false response of 5 ♣ and then raising when partner signs off in five or six diamonds. Here is an example.

♠ 7 6	♠ A K Q 8 4 3	W	E
♡ A 9 6 5 3	♡ K 7	1 ♡	2 ♠
◇ A K 5 2	◇ Q J 9 4	3 ◇	4 NT
♣ A 10	♣ 6	5 ♣	6 ◇
		7 ◇	—

Aware of the risk that 5 ◇ might be passed, West conceals an ace and responds 5 ♣. When East bids the small slam knowing a vital card to be missing, West rediscovers his ace and proceeds to seven.

5 ♡ Response

This is perhaps the most common of the Byzantine responses and certainly one of the most useful. It shows the regulation two aces, or AKQ or AK(K). Note that this is the only response in which the combination K(K) occurs.

When there are two key suits half-key kings are no longer shown, but the response can instead be made with AKK.

♠ A K Q 7 2	♠ 6 5	W	E
♡ 5	♡ A 9 3	1 ♠	2 ◇
◇ A 4 3	◇ K Q 10 8 7 5	3 ♣	3 ◇
♣ K Q 10 8	♣ 7 4	4 NT	5 ♡
		6 ◇	—

West knows that a 5 ♡ response will guarantee a good play for slam, since if an ace is missing it must mean that the trumps are solid.

Thus it can be seen that Byzantine serves as a trump asking bid as well as a means of checking on aces and kings. In effect it harvests the benefits of the grand slam force for small slam purposes.

♠ K 4	♠ A Q J 6 3	W	E
♡ A J 8 4	♡ 7	1 NT	3 ♠
◇ K 7 6 2	◇ A Q 9 5 4	3 NT	4 ◇
♣ Q 9 5	♣ A 3	4 ♡	4 NT
		5 ♡	7 ◇

Here the 5 ♡ response places all the key cards for East and enables him to bid the grand slam with confidence.

♠ A 8 7 5 3	♠ Q J 6 4	W	E
♡ 4	♡ A K Q 10 8	1 ♣	2 ♡
◇ K Q	◇ 5 4	2 ♠	4 ♠
♣ K Q 9 6 3	♣ A 7	4 NT	5 ♡
		5 ♠	—

West knows from the 5 ♡ response that either two aces are missing or else the trumps are shaky. In neither case does he wish to play in slam. The responder should always respect a sign-off after a 5 ♡ response.

5 ♠ Response

This normally shows AA*KQ* or AAA(K). When there are two key suits the response may show AA*KQ*, AA*KK* or A*KQK*. As an aid to memory it is worth noting that the 5 ♠ response always shows four honour cards.

♠ K	♠ A 10 4	W	E
♡ 8 3	♡ A 10 7	1 ◇	3 NT
◇ A 9 8 6 3	◇ K Q 2	4 ♣	4 ♡
♣ A K Q 7 2	♣ J 10 8 5	4 NT	5 ♠
		7 ♣	—

Here there are two key suits and the 5 ♠ response, showing two aces plus the king and queen of diamonds, makes it easy for West to bid the grand slam.

♠ 10 3	♠ A 7	W	E
♡ A K	♡ 9 8 4	1 ◇	3 ♣
◇ K 10 8 7 6 4 3	◇ A J 5 2	3 ◇	4 ◇
♣ Q 4	♣ A K 8 7	4 ♡	4 ♠
		4 NT	5 ♠
		7 NT	—

The 5 ♠ response promises three aces and the king of clubs and West can count thirteen tricks.

♠ A K 7 6 4	♠ Q J 3	W	E
♡ 10 8 3	♡ A 6 2	1 ♠	2 ◇
◇ K 9 6	◇ A Q 8 7 5 2	3 ◇	3 ♠
♣ A 5	♣ 3	4 ♠	4 NT
		5 ♠	7 NT

Note that East is careful to support spades before bidding 4 NT. The creation of a second key suit solves all problems when West is able to show AA*KK*.

♠ K 9	♠ A 6 3	W	E
♡ K Q J 5	♡ A 10 8 4	1 NT	3 ♣
◇ A 8 6 5	◇ 4	3 ◇	3 ♡
♣ K 8 3	♣ A Q J 9 2	4 ♡	4 NT
		5 ♠	7 ♡

Clubs and hearts are both key suits and the 5 ♠ response, showing A*KQK*, is music in East's ears.

5 NT Response

With one key suit this response normally shows AAA*KQ* or AAAA*K*. With two key suits there are five possible combinations —AAA*KQ*, AAA*KK*, AAAA*K*, AA*KQK* and A*KQKQ*. These strong 5 NT responses, which will obviously be a bit of a rarity, always show five honour cards.

An exceptional case is the weak 5 NT response on AA(*K*). In order to avoid ambiguity, a 5 NT response must not be made on AA(*K*) if the responder has shown any great strength in the bidding. He must have limited his hand in some way, perhaps by making a bid at game level. As noted earlier, the 5 NT response may also be made on AA*K* if there is a risk of 5 ♣ being passed.

♠ A K 10 8 5	♠ Q 4	W	E
♡ 10 7 6 5	♡ A K Q 9 8 2	1 ♠	3 ♡
◇ A 7	◇ 3	4 ♡	4 NT
♣ 9 5	♣ K Q 6 2	5 NT	6 ♡

Having limited his hand by making a bid that could have been passed at the game level, West can safely respond 5 NT rather than 5 ♡ on the next round.

This hand from the Bidding Challenge feature in Bridge Magazine is practically tailor-made for Byzantine, although Key-Card Blackwood would get there as well.

		W	E
♠ A K 10 3	♠ Q J 9 2	2 NT	3 ♣
♡ A J 8 4	♡ 3	3 ♡	3 ♠
◇ A 8 3	◇ K Q J 9 2	4 ♣	4 NT
♣ A 4	♣ 8 7 2	5 NT	7 ♠

The cue-bid of four clubs agrees spades, and the Byzantine response of 5 NT shows AAAA*K*. The only significant card that East does not know about is the ten of spades, but he bids the grand slam anyway, realising that at worst it will depend on a 3-2 trump break.

		W	E
♠ A 4 3	♠ K Q 8 7 2	1 ◇	2 ♠
♡ K 8 5 3	♡ A	3 ♠	4 ◇
◇ A Q 10 6 4	◇ K J 7 5	4 NT	5 NT
♣ 6	♣ A 9 4	7 ◇	—

The 5 NT response, showing AA*KQK*, plugs the gaps in West's hand nicely.

Voids

It is inadvisable to bid 4 NT on a hand containing a void unless the void has already been indicated by means of a jump cue-bid.

As always, the ace of a suit in which either partner has made a jump cue-bid is suppressed in responding to 4 NT.

		W	E
♠ A 9 6 4	♠ K Q J 7 5 2	1 ◇	1 ♠
♡ A J 2	♡ K 7	4 ♣	4 NT
◇ A K J 7 6 3	◇ 5	5 ♠	7 ♠
♣ —	♣ Q 8 6 3		

The 5 ♠ response shows AAA(K) outside clubs, the suit in which the jump cue-bid was made.

		W	E
♠ A 9 6 4	♠ K Q J 7 5 2	1 ◇	1 ♠
♡ A J 2	♡ K 7	4 ♣	4 NT
◇ K Q J 7 6	◇ 5	5 ♡	6 ♠
♣ A	♣ Q 8 6 3		

With a different hand West suppresses his ace of clubs, responding 5 ♡ to show two aces outside the club suit.

♠ Q J 10 8 7	♠ A K 6 5 3	W	N	E	S
♡ A 4 2	♡ —	1 ♠	2 ♡	4 ♡	—
◇ Q 10	◇ K J 8 7	4 ♠	—	4 NT	—
♣ A 7 5	♣ K Q 3 2	5 ◇	—	6 ♠	all pass

West discounts the ace of the suit in which his partner is known to be void.

See how Byzantine combines with the jump cue-bid to eliminate guesswork on the Rose-Gardener hand from page 102.

♠ 7 6	♠ A 9	W	N	E	S
♡ —	♡ 10 6 5	1 ◇	1 ♠	3 ♣	—
◇ A 8 6 5 4 2	◇ K Q 7	4 ♡	—	4 NT	—
♣ K Q 9 7 4	♣ A J 8 5 2	5 ♡	—	7 ♣	all pass

The 5 ♡ response shows AKQ in addition to primary heart control, which tells East the whole story.

Voids in Responder's Hand

The responder may show a previously undisclosed void by jumping to the six-level in response to 4 NT. The jump is made in the void suit if this is under the trump suit and in trumps if the void is over the trump suit.

The jump to the six-level implies two aces or AKQ if the responder has bid strongly (i.e. jumped, reversed or forced), and one ace on normal approach bidding.

Holding three aces and a void, the responder should ignore the void and make his normal Byzantine response. Partner is likely to have the other ace anyway.

When holding two aces and a void in normal approach bidding, the responder must anticipate his partner's bid of 4 NT and take evasive action. A jump cue-bid is always a good way out of the predicament.

♠ 7	♠ A 9 8 6 4 3	W	E
♡ K 4	♡ —	1 ◇	1 ♠
◇ K Q J 9 7	◇ A 5 2	3 ♣	4 ♡
♣ A K Q 9 5	♣ J 10 7 6	4 NT	5 ♡
		7 ♣	—

After the jump cue-bid East can relax and make his normal response, which enables West to bid the grand slam.

If East had carelessly raised three clubs to four, however, he would have been left with no way of indicating his full values after 4 NT. A response of 5 ♡ would show two aces but not the void, while a jump to six clubs would show only one ace and a void. In either case the bidding would fizzle out at the six-level. Clearly a certain degree of forethought must be exercised on hands containing voids.

♠ K 9 4	♠ —	W	E
♡ A J 7 6 2	♡ K Q 8 4	1 ♡	3 ♣
◇ A K 6 4	◇ 9 8 7 3	3 ◇	3 ♡
♣ 3	♣ A K Q J 5	4 NT	6 ♡
		7 ♡	—

The jump to six hearts shows the void in spades along with AKQ, and West has an easy task.

Enemy Interference

This is no more and no less troublesome to Byzantine players than it is to others. The general rule, when 4 NT is overcalled, is to pass if the normal response would have been 5 ♣, to bid one step up to indicate a 5 ◇ response, and so on as far as seems safe. Double is in principle for penalties, although it may merely express the inability to find a safe alternative.

♠ A 10 8 7 3	♠ K Q 9 5	W	N	E	S
♡ 4	♡ 10 3	1 ♠	2 ♡	3 ♠	4 ♡
◇ A K Q 7	◇ 9 6 3	4 NT	5 ♡	5 NT	—
♣ K Q 2	♣ A J 8 4	6 ♠	all pass		

Since West can hardly expect more in the way of controls from the limit raise, it is safe for East to show his AKQ and commit his side to slam.

Grand Slam Tries

The Byzantine machinery makes light work of bidding many grand slams that are hard to reach by other methods. But the response to 4 NT does not always give the full picture. Further bidding may be needed to fill in the detail.

The bid of 5 NT is used in three distinct ways.

1. A direct 5 NT, bypassing 4 NT, is the normal grand slam force enquiring about the top honours in trumps. Players who do not have their own favourite scale of responses may care to adopt the one suggested in Chapter Two.

		W	E
♠ A 9 7 6 4	♠ K 8 5 3 2	1 ♠	2 ♠
♡ J 3	♡ —	3 ◇	4 ♡
◇ A K Q 8 4	◇ 7 6 5 3	5 NT	6 ◇
♣ A	♣ 9 8 6 2	7 ♠	—

It is unusual to reach a grand slam after an opening bid of one and a single raise, but there is no law against it. Here the 6 ◇ response to 5 NT shows K x x x x in trumps.

2. 5 NT immediately after the response to 4 NT asks for additional high-card features. Ignoring kings already shown:

K Q x counts as two features (but K Q alone as one).
K counts as one feature.

An unshown key-suit queen may also be counted as a feature, but only in combination with some other feature. If a queen is all that partner needs for a grand slam he will make a different type of try.

The responses are on simple Roman lines.

6 ♣ — no feature or three.
6 ◇ — one or four.
6 ♡ — two.

Clearly if the trump suit is a minor the 5 NT bidder must be sure that no response can embarrass him.

		W	E
♠ 6 5	♠ A K 7	1 ♡	3 ♣
♡ K Q 10 8 6	♡ A 7 3 2	3 ◇	3 ♡
◇ A K 5 4	◇ Q J	4 ♣	4 NT
♣ K 5	♣ A Q 10 6	5 ♠	5 NT
		6 ◇	7 NT

West thoughtfully supports clubs to create a second key suit, and East is able to place the cards shown by the 5 ♠ response as ◇ A, ♡ K Q and ♣ K. The 6 ◇ response to 5 NT shows one additional feature which can only be ◇ K.

3. When the response to 4 NT is followed by cue-bidding, a subsequent bid of 5 NT enquires about the quality of support in the key suits. The responder is expected to bid the grand slam with anything extra, such as five-card trump support or an unshown queen.

At the Eastbourne Spring Foursomes in 1966 the Sharples brothers had an early success with Byzantine on the following hand.

♠ 5	♠ A 10 4	W	E
♡ Q 10 6	♡ A K 8 5	1 ♣	2 ♡
◇ A 7 5 4	◇ 3	3 ♡	4 ♣
♣ A K 9 8 4	♣ Q 10 7 6 3	4 ◇	4 NT
		5 ♣	5 ◇
		5 ♠	5 NT
		7 ♣	—

After two suits had been agreed, West might himself have bid 4 NT and obtained the necessary information. He chose to cue-bid in diamonds, however, and his partner started the machinery. The 5 ♣ response indicated AA*K*, 5 ◇ and 5 ♠ showed second-round controls, and 5 NT asked for something extra in the key suits.

Having specifically denied a king-queen holding in either suit by his 5 ♣ response, West knew that East must hold both the king of hearts and the queen of clubs for his grand slam try. The only key card unaccounted for was the queen of hearts, and West confidently bid the grand slam on the strength of it.

When there is no room for cue-bidding between 4 NT and 5 NT, the quality of trump support can be queried by the Baron grand slam try—a bid of six in the unbid suit immediately below trumps.

♠ A Q 5	♠ K J 10 9 3	W	E
♡ A J 10 8 4	♡ K	1 ♡	2 ♠
◇ J 6 3	◇ A 8	3 ♠	4 NT
♣ 7 4	♣ A K Q 9 5	5 ♡	6 ◇
		7 ♠	—

Here the 5 ♡ response leaves no space for cue-bidding. East does not bid 5 NT, for he is not interested in any additional tricks his partner may have in diamonds. All he needs to know about is the queen of trumps, and the bid of 6 ◇ asks the right question.

5 NT is by no means the only grand slam try that is available. Byzantine is at its best when used in conjunction with high-level cue-bidding.

♠ A Q 7	♠ K J 10 6 2	W	E
♡ A 9 7 4	♡ Q 3	1 ◇	2 ♠
◇ A J 10 9 3	◇ K Q 5	3 ♠	4 ◇
♣ 5	♣ A Q 4	4 NT	5 ♠
		6 ♣	7 ♠

The response of 5 ♠ strongly suggests the possibility of a grand slam. West cannot quite count thirteen tricks and, rather than bid 5 NT, decides to show his second-round club control. Having told the full story about his spade and diamond honours, East knows that West must have the queen of spades for his grand slam try. That is all he needs to know.

Here is a Roman 2 ◇ auction.

♠ A K J 6	♠ Q 10 8	W	E
♡ A J 6 5	♡ 2	2 ◇	2 NT(1)
◇ A K J 4	◇ 10 8 7 6 5 2	3 ♣(2)	3 ◇(3)
♣ 3	♣ A Q 2	4 ♣(4)	4 ◇(5)
		4 ♠(6)	4 NT
		5 ◇(7)	5 ♡(8)
		5 ♠(8)	7 ◇

(1) Positive response.
(2) Shortage.
(3) Natural. The trump suit.
(4) 4-4-4-1 shape with good controls and good trumps.
(5) Awaiting encouragement.
(6) Encouragement in the form of a cue-bid.
(7) Showing AAA*K*.
(8) Second-round controls.

Note that East would not have learned what he needed to know if he had bid 5 NT over 5 ◇. The response of 6 ◇, showing one additional feature, would have left him in doubt as to whether there was a spade loser or not.

Immediate 4 NT

You may have noticed that none of the examples in this chapter has featured a response of 4 NT on the first round of bidding. There is a good reason for this. It is recommended that a jump to 4 NT on the first round of bidding be treated as Blackwood, not Byzantine.

The opener is expected to show his aces on the normal Blackwood schedule. The immediate jump to 4 NT does not imply support for the opener's suit, and the responder alone will fix the level and the denomination of the final contract. The idea is to eliminate ambiguity on the rare occasions when the responder holds something like the following hand.

♠ A K Q 10 7	♠ 3	W	E
♡ 6	♡ A K Q J 9 8 5 4	1 ♠	4 NT
◇ K J 5 3	◇ A	5 ◇	6 ♡
♣ 9 7 3	♣ K Q J		

For West the message of the immediate jump to 4 NT is: "Forget about your king and queen of spades and just tell me how many aces you have."

If East had forced in hearts and bid 4 NT on the second round he would have agreed spades by implication. The Byzantine response of 5 ♡ would then have left him unsure of whether an ace was missing or not.

The first-round jump to 4 NT is analogous to the Acol opening bid of 4 NT. In both cases the 4 NT bidder is interested in nothing but aces.

The only occasion when Byzantine is used on the first round of bidding is after an opening bid at the four-level, e.g. 4 ♡–4 NT. Now there can be no ambiguity regarding aces, and it is useful for the responder to be able to check up on trump solidity.

After 2 ♣

When one partner is powerful enough to open with a game-forcing bid it is unlikely that the other will be over-endowed with aces and kings. It therefore makes sense to modify the responses to 4 NT to enable the partner of the 2 ♣ bidder to show weaker values.

Two separate scales of modified responses are recommended, depending on whether the opening bid of 2 ♣ elicits a positive or a negative response.

The assumption is that natural responses to 2 ♣ are used, a positive response being made on any hand containing:

(a) an ace and a king.
(b) eight points with either one ace or two kings.
(c) six or seven points including at least one king and a good five-card suit.

The responses to a subsequent bid of 4 NT by the opener are as follows:

	After Negative	After Positive
5 ♣ —	no controls	K
5 ♢ —	K	KK
5 ♡ —	KK	A plus
5 ♠ —	A	AK or KKK
5 NT—	A plus	AA, AKK or KKKK

There is one other situation in which modified responses to 4 NT are made. When the responder is known to have no ace (e.g. after the Acol sequence 2 ♠-4 ♠) he shows his kings in response to 4 NT on the normal Roman schedule.

> 5 ♣ — none or three.
> 5 ♢ — one or four.
> 5 ♡ — two.

These modifications can, of course, be applied to any 4 NT convention. They are not an essential part of Byzantine, although they have been used with success for many years by Jack Marx and the Sharples brothers.

In the light of my own experience I can promise that anyone who gives Byzantine a serious trial will not regret it. Slams that once seemed beyond reach have become a matter of routine.

8 · Asking the Way

Asking bids, developed by Ely Culbertson from an original idea of Albert Morehead's, were introduced to the bridge-playing public in 1936. Although creating an intense flurry of interest at the time, they were not widely adopted. The mass of bridge players rejected them because of the apparent complexity of the responses, the experts because they detected certain basic weaknesses in the method.

The principle of asking for information about controls had previously been confined to the generalised questions asked by the four and five no trump conventions. Culbertson's asking bids were revolutionary in that they used the bid of a new suit at the four-level to ask for specific controls in that and other suits. Such an innovation was clearly incompatible with cue-bidding, and the experts of the day were not prepared to abandon the cue-bids that lay at the heart of their traditional methods.

The big advantage claimed for cue-bidding is that it makes it possible to show a control below game level, thus suggesting a slam to partner and inviting him to express an opinion. He may do this by signing off in trumps, by going straight to slam, by checking on controls in bulk or by making a cue-bid in return. Emphasis is laid on the principle of consultation, whereby both partners play a role in determining the level of the final contract.

Consulting partner involves relying on his judgement, however, and players tend to forget how easy it is for errors of judgement to creep in when the pressure is on. Cue-bidders explain away their bad results by pointing out that it was the players that failed, not the method. After the event it is always possible to produce a cue-bidding sequence that would have led to a happy ending. But can a method that depends so much on good judgement be altogether sound?

With asking bids the one-sided nature of the dialogue comes in for a certain amount of criticism. It is true that the asking bidder has no way of suggesting a slam to his partner: all he can do is ask direct questions about controls. On borderline hands a player must take a view as to whether he is near enough to the slam zone to risk starting an asking sequence which, if positive responses are received, may carry him too high under its own momentum. It cannot be denied that certain hands are awkward for asking bidders, but there is a compensating advantage. When the hands are suitable the slam is reached almost automatically. Judgement is to a large extent replaced by method, thus minimizing the possibility of human error.

Although asking bids did not meet with general approval they were not without their champions in 1936. They were enthusiastically adopted by Dr. Paul Stern and incorporated into the Vienna system, which enjoyed a good deal of success and popularity in the decade that followed. Colonies of asking bidders have survived and multiplied in Central and Eastern Europe, Scandinavia, India, Australia and South Africa. It is perhaps significant that asking bidders tend to remain faithful to their method. Amongst their ranks defection to the enemy is rare to the point of non-existence.

Even in Britain and the United States, where asking bids have long been defunct, there are signs of a revival of interest. No doubt this can be attributed to the slam-bidding successes achieved by Italian and other European systems which make use of rigorously-disciplined question and answer routines.

It is in South Africa that asking bids have found their staunchest advocates. Today the world's leading authorities on the subject are the Sapire brothers—Leon of Johannesburg and Max of East London. Over the years they have done a great deal to modify and streamline Culbertson's original ideas and have emerged with a modern and highly effective method of slam bidding.

It is the "Sapire Variations" that are presented in this chapter.

What is an Asking Bid?

An asking bid may be either:

(1) The bid of a new suit at the four-level after trump agreement.

e.g.	W	E		W	E
	1 ♠	3 ♠		1 ♡	2 ◇
	4 ◇?			3 ◇	4 ♣?

(2) A double jump at the three or four-level, which agrees the last-bid suit by inference.

e.g.

W	E		W	E
1 ♡	3 ♠ ?		1 ♢	1 ♠
			4 ♣ ?	

(3) The bid of a new suit at the four-level by a responder who has forced.

e.g.

W	E		W	E
1 ♡	2 ♠		1 ♠	3 ♣
3 ♡	4 ♣ ?		3 ♠	4 ♡ ?

In both cases the asking bid agrees the opener's suit.

(4) A jump in an opponent's suit, or the bid of an opponent's suit at the four-level without a jump.

e.g.

W	N	E		W	N	E
1 ♢	1 ♡	3 ♡ ?		1 ♣	3 ♠	4 ♠ ?

There may be one or two other situations where by partnership agreement a bid may be treated as an asking bid, but the above will do to be going on with.

The Responses

Primary controls (aces and voids) and secondary controls (kings and singletons) are shown in accordance with the following schedule.

Control in asked suit	Controls elsewhere	Action
None	Immaterial	Sign off in trumps
Secondary	No primary	Sign off in trumps
Secondary	Primary	Bid primary suit (jump if this is trumps)
Primary	No primary	Raise asked suit
Ace	Void	Jump in void suit
Void	Ace	Jump in ace suit
Ace	Ace	Bid no trumps
Secondary	2 Aces	Bid no trumps
Ace	2 Aces	Jump in no trumps
Secondary	3 Aces	Jump in no trumps

For the purposes of a no trump response, a void must not be counted as an ace, although a void in the asked suit may be treated as a secondary control.

Outside voids additional to the above holdings cannot be shown immediately. With secondary control in the asked suit plus an ace and a void elsewhere, for instance, bid the ace suit and hope to be able to show the void later.

Readers wishing to familiarise themselves with the method might care to test themselves on the following example hands. In each case pick a response for East after the sequence:

$$
\begin{array}{cc}
W & E \\
1\spadesuit & 2\heartsuit \\
4\clubsuit? & ?
\end{array}
$$

(a) ♠ J 6
♡ A 10 9 6 5 2
♢ A 3
♣ Q 10 5

(b) ♠ 7 4
♡ K Q J 6 5 4
♢ K Q 8
♣ K 6

(c) ♠ —
♡ Q J 9 8 7 4
♢ K Q J 4
♣ K 7 2

(d) ♠ 9
♡ K J 9 8 3
♢ J 6 3
♣ A Q 8 6

(e) ♠ 8 6 5
♡ A Q 10 7 4 3
♢ K 9 5
♣ 6

(f) ♠ Q 6 5
♡ K 10 8 5 3 2
♢ —
♣ A 8 5 3

(g) ♠ A 5
♡ J 10 8 7 6 3
♢ K Q 9 5 2
♣ —

(h) ♠ 7
♡ Q J 8 6 4 3
♢ A 9 6 3
♣ A J

(i) ♠ A 2
♡ A J 10 7 4
♢ 10 7 6 2
♣ K Q

(j) ♠ A 10 4
♡ A 9 7 6 4 2
♢ Q 9 8 5
♣ —

(k) ♠ 5
♡ A J 7 6 2
♢ A 4 3
♣ A 9 6 5

(l) ♠ A 6
♡ A 8 7 6 4 3
♢ A 7 5 4
♣ J

Answers

(a) 4 ♡. Although he has a fair hand East lacks club control and must therefore sign off.

(b) 4 ♡. Secondary club control is present, but this time East has to sign off for want of a primary control.

(c) 4 ♠. With secondary club control, East can show his primary control in spades.

(*d*) 5 ♣. East raises the asked suit to indicate that his only primary control is in clubs.

(*e*) 5 ♡. The jump in trumps shows secondary club control plus the ace of trumps.

(*f*) 5 ◇. The jump in a side suit shows an ace in the asked suit and a void in the bid suit, or vice versa. This differs from the Culbertson treatment, where the jump in a side suit indicated a hand containing two aces and a void.

(*g*) 5 ♠. Again an ace and a void. In practice it has been found that the asker can normally tell which is the void suit and which the ace. If in doubt he can make a further asking bid to find out.

(*h*) 4 NT. A hand with two aces, one of which is in the asked suit.

(*i*) 4 NT. Again two aces, this time with secondary control in the asked suit.

(*j*) 4 NT. The void in the asked suit is treated as a secondary control for the meantime. It may be possible to show it later.

(*k*) 5 NT. The jump in no trumps always indicates a three-ace hand.

(*l*) 5 NT. Again three aces, this time with secondary control in the asked suit.

Subsequent Asking Bids

1. After a negative response a further asking bid in a new suit asks the same questions. The responder replies exactly as he would have done to an original asking bid in this suit.

A repeat asking bid in the same suit after a negative response is concerned only with second-round control. Without it the responder again signs off in trumps. With second-round control in the asked suit, the responder bids a side-suit in which he holds a further second-round control or, lacking this, bids no trumps.

The above differs from the Culbertson treatment, in which the responder was requested to show a primary control if he had third-round control in the asked suit.

2. After a positive response any further asking bid, including a repeat asking bid in the same suit, is for the next control in line. This will be second-round or third-round control depending on what the responder has already shown in the suit. The responder admits possession of this control by showing an additional "next

control", or bidding no trumps if he has nothing else to show. As always, the sign-off in the trump suit denies the required control.

Although the asker is presumed to be satisfied about the primary control position, the responder may still indicate a void in the asked suit by raising.

A third asking bid is normally for third-round control, as is any asking bid made at the six-level.

Norman 4 NT

This convention fits nicely into the asking structure. A bid of 4 NT is treated as Norman in two situations.

(1) Before any asking bid has been made.
(2) After a negative response to an asking bid.

Trump Asking Bid

After a positive response to an asking bid, a bid of no trumps at the cheapest level is Culbertson's Trump Asking Bid for top trump honours. In response to a TAB of 4 NT.

> 5 ♣ — shows no top honour.
> 5 ◇ — shows one.
> 5 ♡ — shows two.
> 5 ♠ — shows all three.

A further TAB of 5 NT now queries trump length, the responses being:

> 6 ♣ — three or fewer.
> 6 ◇ — four.
> 6 ♡ — five or six.
> 6 ♠ — seven or more.

When the response to the initial asking bid takes the bidding beyond 4 NT, 5 NT is used to check on trump honours, and if 5 NT itself is crowded out 6 ♣ is used for the same purpose (although not when clubs are trumps, obviously).

That is enough theory for now. Let us have a look at some example hands.

Leon Sapire's interest in asking bids was first awakened more

I

than twenty years ago when he watched two expert players, using traditional cue-bidding methods, stop in six spades on the following cards.

♠ A K Q 10 7 3   ♠ J 9 6 2
♡ 5   ♡ A 7 6 3
♢ A 3   ♢ K 9 4
♣ A K 4 3   ♣ 7 5

Now it is possible, as always, to construct cue-bidding sequences to reach the grand slam. Starting with the forcing two-bid in vogue at the time:

W	E		W	E
2 ♠	3 ♠	or	2 ♠	3 ♠
4 ♣	4 ♡		4 ♢	4 ♡
5 ♣	5 ♢		5 ♣	5 ♢
5 ♡	6 ♣		5 ♡	5 ♠
7 ♠	—		6 ♣	7 ♠

The above sequences are reasonable enough, but vital judgement decisions are required from both players. West has to organise his bidding so as to make maximum use of the available space, and East has to realise that his doubleton club is the key feature. It is all too easy to go astray.

On testing the asking bids, Leon Sapire discovered that the grand slam practically bid itself. Here is the asking sequence.

W	E
2 ♠	3 ♠
4 ♢ ?	4 ♡
5 ♣ ?	5 ♠
6 ♣ ?	6 NT
7 ♠	—

The question marks are merely to indicate, for the benefit of those unfamiliar with the method, which bids are asking bids. They do not imply, as a correspondent once suggested, that asking bids should be made with a rising inflection of the voice.

After discovering that East has secondary diamond and primary heart control, West makes a further asking bid in clubs. East denies second-round control by signing off in five spades, but on the next round admits to his third-round club control. What could be simpler?

In the above example the asking style results in an auction that is free from strain, and this is no isolated case. A similar effect can be observed on many hands.

	♠ 3		♠ A K Q J 4
	♡ A J 7 6 5 2		♡ K Q 10 3
	◇ A 3		◇ 10 6 4
	♣ J 8 7 4		♣ 9

Cue-Bidding		*Asking*	
W	E	W	E
1 ♡	2 ♠	1 ♡	4 ◇ ?
3 ♡	4 ♡	4 NT	6 ♡
5 ◇	6 ♡		

The cue-bidders reach the slam when West displays good judgement in bidding on beyond the level of game. In practice many players would pass four hearts, fearing three quick losers in clubs.

In the asking sequence East goes straight to the crux of the matter when he queries his partner's diamond holding. The response of four no trumps, showing two aces with first or second-round diamond control, tells him that there is likely to be a good play for six and no play for seven.

Asking can also be effective in keeping the bidding low when no slam is on. In the U.S. Olympiad Trials of 1964 six out of eight pairs bid to a hopeless slam on the following cards.

	♠ 3 2		♠ Q 8 5
	♡ A Q 5 4		♡ K J 9 3
	◇ A K Q 9 6 2		◇ 4 3
	♣ 9		♣ A K 7 2

Cue-Bidding		*Asking*	
W	E	W	E
1 ◇	1 ♡	1 ◇	1 ♡
4 ♡	5 ♣	3 ♠ ?	4 ♡
5 ◇	5 ♡	—	
—			

Disciplined cue-bidders can stop at the five-level, but that may be too high if both red suits break badly.

In the asking sequence the bidding automatically dies at the four-level when West receives a negative response to his spade enquiry.

No method is better than asking for detecting duplication of values at a safe level.

		W	E
♠ 5	♠ A K Q J 8	1 ♡	2 ♠
♡ K J 10 7 4 3	♡ A Q 6	3 ♡	4 ◇ ?
◇ Q J 9	◇ 8 7 3	4 ♡	—
♣ K Q 5	♣ A 10		

East is ready for great adventures but is stopped in his tracks by the negative response to his asking bid in diamonds.

On this hand from the South African Open Team Championship of 1970, Mick Haddad and Max Sapire earned a big swing for their team.

		W	E
♠ J 10 8 7 6	♠ A K Q 9	(Haddad)	(Sapire)
♡ A K 5 3	♡ 10 8 7 6	1 ♠	4 ◇ ?
◇ K 4	◇ A 9 6	4 ♡	5 ♡ ?
♣ J 7	♣ A K	5 NT	6 ♡ ?
		6 ♣	—

The opponents in the other room, having located the 5-4 spade fit and all the aces and kings, bid gaily to seven.

Sapire stopped in six when he discovered that his partner lacked third-round control in hearts. Although it was just possible for West to have held a singleton diamond and four clubs headed by the queen and knave, the grand slam was clearly against the odds when third-round heart control was known to be missing.

The Asking Suit

The factors that govern the choice of asking suit are fairly obvious from the first few examples. The asking bid is normally made in the cheapest suit in which a control is needed to give the slam a chance.

♠ A J 8 6 4	♠ K 10 9 3 2	*W*	*E*
♡ A K	♡ Q J 3	1 ♠	4 ♡ ?
◇ 8 5 2	◇ K Q 6 4	4 NT	6 ♠
♣ 10 9 8	♣ A		

The heart suit is chosen as the asking suit, since East does not need club or diamond controls from his partner. Once he is assured of two aces and heart control in the West hand the slam becomes a reasonable proposition.

But it will often be right to ask in a suit in which first-round control is held, particularly when the suit contains a couple of losers.

♠ K	♠ A 9 5 4	*W*	*E*
♡ A Q 10 5 3 2	♡ K 9 8 6	1 ♡	3 ♡
◇ A 7 6 3	◇ 4	4 ◇ ?	4 ♠
♣ K 4	♣ J 10 9 8	5 ◇ ?	5 NT
		6 ♡	—

Here diamonds is the right asking suit, since second-round diamond control is vital for slam purposes. When East admits to this and the ace of spades, a further ask in diamonds locates third-round control in the suit. West is unable to check the trump position but knows that at worst the slam will depend on a trump finesse.

Which Hand Should Ask

The question of which hand should assume the captaincy by starting an asking sequence will often be determined by random factors such as the position of the dealer. On many hands it will not matter which partner does the asking. When there is a choice, however, the more distributional hand should do the asking for it will have fewer holes to fill.

To digress for a moment, asking bids were designed to fit the framework of the Culbertson system, which incorporated the forcing double raise and other adjuncts of what is now known as Standard American. In spite of this, asking bids can be used equally well by Acol players, although traditionalists may shudder at the clash of philosophies.

Players who use limit raises in the major suits will feel the need for some kind of forcing raise, however, and a conventional response of three no trumps is usually chosen for this purpose.

		W	E
♠ A Q 8 6 5 2	♠ K 9 7 4	1 ♠	3 NT
♡ K 10	♡ A 4 3	4 ♣?	4 NT
◇ 7	◇ A 10 6 3	5 ♣?	5 NT
♣ A J 7 2	♣ K 8	6 ♣?	6 ♡
		7 ♠	—

Semi-balanced hands such as East's are generally better asked about than asking. The three no trump reponse gives the message of good controls and trump support and invites West to start an asking sequence. West asks twice in clubs and discovers his partner to have two aces along with second and third-round control of clubs. Five no trumps having been crowded out, six clubs is used as the TAB, and the response of six hearts shows one top trump honour to complete the picture.

It is in the bidding of distributional grand slams such as this that asking bids are seen at their best. Note the value of the repeat ask to check on the next control in clubs. It would hardly be possible to reach seven without this feature.

Voids

This is not such an abrupt change of subject as it may appear to be, for Culbertson used the repeat ask after a no trump response as a request for clarification of the aces held. In South Africa this treatment was abandoned on grounds of frequency in favour of asking for the control next in line as in the last example hand.

There is an occasional difficulty when a void is held however. Sometimes it is possible to get around the problem by asking in the void suit itself.

		W	E
♠ K Q J 8 7 3	♠ A 9 6 2	2 ♠	3 ♠
♡ K Q	♡ A 9 3	4 ◇?	4 ♠
◇ —	◇ J 7 6 3	4 NT?	5 ♡
♣ K Q J 10 4	♣ 8 5	6 ♣	—

When East supports spades the best West can do is to ask in diamonds and hope for a negative reply. If it comes he uses

Norman to discover how many working aces his partner holds and places the contract accordingly.

Clearly this is not completely satisfactory, for a no trump response leaves West in a guessing situation while a diamond raise carries him overboard.

♠ Q 10 6 5	♠ —	W	E
♡ A 7	♡ K Q 10 6	1 ♣	3 ♠ ?
◇ K Q 5	◇ A J 8 3	4 ♣	4 ◇ ?
♣ A 9 8 3	♣ K Q J 6 4	4 NT	5 ◇ ?
		5 ♠	7 ♣

After asking in the void suit and hearing a sign-off, East hits the jackpot when he tries again in diamonds. The repeat ask in diamonds is for third-round control, and West affirms this by showing his queen of spades *en passant*.

Note that the responder to a subsequent asking bid is always required to show "next control" in a side suit if he possesses it. No trumps is used as the positive response only when no outside control can be shown. In the above case the queen of spades can be shown because West has already denied first or second-round control in the suit. West also has third-round control of hearts, but that is not the "next control" in the suit since he has neither affirmed nor denied second-round control of hearts.

As it happens the spade queen is redundant, but the knowledge that West has third-round diamond control enables East to bid the grand slam. Once again, however, he was lucky in receiving a negative response to his asking bid in spades. If West had held the king of spades his response would have been four no trumps, and East would have been unable to discover whether or not the right aces were held.

The South Africans may feel the loss of the repeat ask to clarify aces on certain hands, but there can be little doubt that they gain heavily on balance by using the repeat ask to query the next control in the suit.

A void may be disclosed at a later stage if a subsequent asking bid is made in the suit.

♠ K 5 3	♠ A 9 4	W	E
♡ A 10 8 7 3	♡ K 9 6 5 4	1 ♡	3 ♠ ?
◇ A J 9 6 2	◇ K	3 NT	4 ♣ ?
♣ —	♣ A J 6 3	5 ♣	7 ♡

The asking bid in clubs is for second-round control, but West indicates his void by raising. Knowing that his partner cannot have less than five hearts, East does not need to ask about trumps.

Conservation of Bidding Space

The last hand illustrates a further point about the choice of asking suit. Asking bids are in general economical of bidding space, since several features can be shown in the one response. However, it is always possible to run out of space if the first asking bid is chosen unwisely.

In the last example, expecting a positive response to any asking bid he makes, East chooses spades for reasons of economy. If by any chance West has to sign off in four hearts East can always try again with five clubs. If East had asked first in clubs, however, the bidding would have proceeded in one of three ways.

(a) W	E	(b) W	E	(c) W	E
1 ♡	4 ♣ ?	1 ♡	4 ♣ ?	1 ♡	4 ♣ ?
4 NT	5 ♠ ?	4 NT	5 ♣ ?	4 NT	5 ♣ ?
6 ♣	?	6 ♣	?	5 ♠	5 NT ?
				6 ◇	?

In sequence (a) East hears about the two aces, second-round control of spades and second and third-round control of clubs. He cannot be sure that West has five trumps, however. West could well have a 1-4-4-4 or 4-4-4-1 shape, and the grand slam is too much of a gamble.

Sequence (b) serves no better. East knows his partner to have five trumps but has not heard about the vital second-round control in spades.

In sequence (c) West keeps quiet about the void in clubs in order to show his spade control. Now there is room for a TAB, but the response denies the queen of trumps and leaves East no further forward.

Clearly it is in this area—making optimum use of the available bidding space—that the greatest calls are made on the judgement of the asking bidder.

♠ Q 10 7 6 2	♠ A K 9 3	W	E
♡ A 3	♡ K J 5 2	1 ♠	3 NT
◇ A K	◇ 10 9 5	4 NT?	5 ♠
♣ A 9 5 4	♣ K 8	6 ♣?	6 NT
		7 ♠	—

Although West needs to know the club position, he postpones his asking bid in clubs until he has discovered via Norman that his partner holds an ace and three kings. Third-round club control is then the only feature left to investigate.

If West had asked first in clubs the expected response of five spades would have carried the bidding too high too soon, leaving insufficient space to check on third-round club control, the king of hearts *and* the king of trumps.

♠ K Q 9 6 5 4	♠ A J 10 3	W	E
♡ A 6 5 2	♡ 9	1 ♠	3 NT
◇ 7	◇ A 10 6 3	4 ♡?	4 NT
♣ A 2	♣ K 9 8 4	5 ♡?	6 ♣
		7 ♠	—

As it happens West would have reached the grand slam just as easily if he had made his second asking bid in clubs. That would have been a poor effort, however, since the king of clubs is not an essential card. What West needs to find in his partner's hand is third-round heart control along with either minor suit king, and the repeat ask in hearts is the correct move.

Trump Asking Bid

The following hand is not well suited to the asking style, but when a cue-bid comes to the rescue the trump asking bid combines with Norman to do the rest.

♠ A K Q	♠ J 10 8 6 5 3	W	E
♡ A 9 5	♡ K Q J 7 4 3	1 NT	3 ♠
◇ J 9 6 2	◇ A	4 ♡	4 NT?
♣ Q 10 7	♣ —	5 ♠	5 NT?
		6 ♠	7 ♠

This is the only situation in which the Sapire brothers admit the use of a cue-bid. Four hearts is a cue-bid raise, showing spade support and the ace of hearts and naturally denying a lower-ranking ace. From the Norman response of five spades East can deduce that his partner has at least the king in trumps. This makes it safe to introduce the TAB, which hits the jackpot when West is able to show all three top honours.

The cue-bid raise is very necessary in this case. If West merely raises to four spades, East cannot safely ask in hearts lest a no trump response take him too high when the ace and king of spades are missing.

In passing it is worth noting that Byzantine, with its in-built TAB element, gobbles up the hand in three rounds.

Asking bidders have to stick to Norman, however. As is customary with Norman users, a hand that has opened with a strong bid such as two no trumps is assumed to hold a minimum of three aces or the equivalent. Thus the five-club response shows no more than three aces, the five-diamond response three and a half, and so on.

♠ A Q 5	♠ 9 4	W	E
♡ K 8 3	♡ A Q 10 6 4 2	2 NT	3 ◇
◇ A K 7 3	◇ 5	3 ♡	4 NT?
♣ A 9 6	♣ K Q J 2	5 ♡	5 NT?
		6 ◇	7 NT

When the transfer bid of three diamonds is followed by Norman, West responds five hearts to show the equivalent of four aces. This allows room for the TAB to check on the king of trumps.

The TAB extension for trump length can be useful on hands like the following.

♠ 7	♠ A J 4	W	E
♡ A 7 6 2	♡ K J 10 8 4 3	1 ◇	2 ♡
◇ A K J 9 3	◇ 8 4	3 ♡	3 ♠ ?
♣ J 8 3	♣ A K	3 NT	4 ◇ ?
		4 ♠	4 NT ?
		5 ◇	5 NT ?
		6 ◇	7 ♡

Having located two aces, second and third-round spade control and the king of diamonds in his partner's hand, East asks for trump honours. It is disappointing when West denies the queen, but East asks again and finds his partner with the four-card trump length that makes the grand slam a good proposition.

Responding on a "Weak" Hand

When the responder to an asking bid has previously denied strength (by making a negative response to an opening bid of two clubs, for instance) the two-ace requirement for a no trump response becomes redundant. In such cases the no trump response merely affirms second-round control in the asked suit. With second-round control and an outside ace the normal response is given.

A hand that opens with a pre-emptive bid can safely be included in the "weak" category.

♠ K 6	♠ A 9 8 5 4	W	E
♡ K J 9 8 6 3 2	♡ A Q 7 5	3 ♡	4 ♠ ?
◇ J 9 3	◇ —	4 NT	5 ♣ ?
♣ 5	♣ A Q 8 2	5 ♠	5 NT ?
		6 ◇	7 ♡

When East discovers his partner to have second and third-round control of spades, second-round control of clubs and the king of hearts, he knows the grand slam must be cold.

When the responder has denied an ace, as in the Acol sequence 2 ♠-4 ♠, he shows an additional second-round control if he possesses it.

♠ A 10 4	♠ K 8	*W*	*E*
♡ A K Q 7 6 3	♡ 10 9 5 2	2 ♡	4 ♡
◇ —	◇ J 8 3 2	4 ♠?	5 ♣
♣ A 9 6 4	♣ K Q 5	5 ♠?	6 ♣
		7 ♡	—

The responses locate second and third-round controls in both black suits, which is just what West needs.

Asking for a Lead

Critics of the asking style make much of the point that a negative response often tells the defenders what to lead. Asking bidders do not find this too serious a disadvantage, however, for there is ample compensation on hands like the following.

♠ A K 9 7 6 3	♠ J 10 8 4	*W*	*E*
♡ K 10 7 4	♡ A 8 3	1 ♠	3 ♠
◇ 6	◇ A 10 3 2	4 ♣?	4 ♠
♣ A Q	♣ 7 5	4 NT?	5 ♡
		6 ♠	—

It is comforting for West to know that the contemptuous gentleman on his left is likely to lead a club.

Enemy Interference

Opponents who double asking bids present the responder with an extra option—that of redoubling to indicate second-round control in the asked suit with no primary controls outside. Also, since a pass now serves as the negative response, it is no longer necessary to jump in trumps to show the ace. All other responses remain the same after a double.

Enemy overcalls at a low level do not preclude the use of asking bids.

♠ A Q 9 5 3	♠ K J 7 4 2	*W*	*N*	*E*	*S*
♡ A 10 6	♡ 4				
◇ 9	◇ A 10 7 6 4 3	1 ♠	2 ♡	4 ◇?	4 ♡
♣ Q 8 5 2	♣ 6	4 NT	—	6 ♠	all
					pass

The jump to four diamonds remains an asking bid since the overcall in the opponent's suit is available as a general force.

Asking bids are abandoned and all bids become natural, however, when the opponents intervene at the three-level or higher. An exception to this rule is that a bid of the enemy suit at the four-level or higher is always an asking bid.

Jump Asking Bids

Many jumps are asking bids, but they are defined as jump asking bids only when the bid of the suit at a lower level would itself have been an asking bid. The jump asking bid expresses interest in nothing but third-round controls.

♠ A K 4	♠ Q 9 6	*W*	*E*
♡ A K 7	♡ Q 3 2	2 ♣	2 ◇
◇ A K Q J 6 2	◇ 9 8 7 4	3 ◇	4 ◇
♣ A	♣ 10 7 3	5 ♡?	5 ♠
		7 ◇	—

West decides to play in six and tries a jump ask in hearts on the way. East affirms third-round control in both hearts and spades and the grand slam is reached. West is unable to bid seven no trumps, for he does not know whether his partner is showing queens or doubletons. East could equally well have held either of the following hands.

♠ 9 6	or	♠ 9 6
♡ Q 3 2		♡ 3 2
◇ 9 8 7 4		◇ 9 8 7 4 3
♣ 10 7 3 2		♣ 10 7 3 2

This inability to distinguish between control by strength and control by shortage is a minor defect of the asking method. Not that it is likely to matter very much whether a successful grand slam is played in no trumps or a suit. The ambiguity is more serious when a player cannot tell whether it is the ace or a void opposite his five cards headed by the king and queen.

Advanced Asking Inferences

It may not have occurred to you that there is another holding that fits East's bidding on the previous hand.

♠ A K 4	♠ 9 6 5	W	E
♡ A K 7	♡ Q 3	2 ♣	2 ◇
◇ A K Q J 6 2	◇ 9 8 7 4	3 ◇	4 ◇
♣ A	♣ 10 7 3 2	5 ♡ ?	5 ♠
		7 ◇	—

How can East show third-round spade control when he does not possess it? Well, if you look a little more closely into the position you will see that East does, in effect, have third-round spade control. He knows that his partner must hold at least ace, king and another heart to express an interest in third-round control of the suit. It follows that one of East's spades can be discarded on the third round of hearts, giving third-round control of spades as well.

East cannot tell, of course, whether his imaginative effort will be of any help to his partner. All he knows is that if West needs third-round spade control he has it.

Here is a further example of this type of inference.

♠ A K 5	♠ J 9 6 4 3	W	E
♡ 9 7 3	♡ A	1 ◇	3 ♠ ?
◇ A Q 9 5 4	◇ K J 8 2	3 NT	4 ♠ ?
♣ Q 8	♣ A K 4	4 NT	5 ♣ ?
		5 ♠	5 NT?
		6 ♡	7 ◇

Having discovered that West holds two aces and second-round spade control, East makes his next asking bid in clubs for reasons of economy. Since the four no trump response denied a second-round control other than in spades, the club ask is for third-round control. Holding queen and another, West realises that his spade loser will disappear on the third round of clubs and therefore shows control in both suits. All that remains is for East to check the trumps.

Note that if West lacks third-round control in clubs and signs off in five diamonds there is still room for East to ask about third-round spade control, with the TAB of six clubs in reserve when he receives a favourable response.

That ends my summary of the asking principles used and advocated by Leon and Max Sapire. I think you will agree that the material in this chapter amounts to a complete and formidable slam-bidding method which can be expected to achieve a high degree of accuracy, particularly in the grand slam zone.

By present day standards the responses to asking bids are far from difficult. Do not let yourself be deterred from trying the method on this account. The tournament players of today are accustomed to unravelling far greater complexities in the codified sequences of the Italian systems.

Personally I might be persuaded to abandon cue-bids for asking bids but for the fact that I would have to give up Super Swiss, jump cue-bids and Byzantine as well. The full price seems a little too high.

9 · Asking Around the World

Many variations on the Culbertson asking theme are played in remote corners of the world, and certain systems of foreign origin use asking bids of a completely different type. We cannot hope to examine every variation, but some are required reading for any slam-bidding course. So come with me on a short guided tour.

AUSTRALIA

Australian asking methods adhere more closely to the original Culbertson ideas, but there are several important differences. The New South Wales system, used so successfully by Australian players in recent World Championship and Olympiad events, traces its ancestry back to Vienna. It is therefore natural that asking bids should be part of the design. Two clubs is used as the forcing opening bid instead of the one no trump of Vienna, and a forcing opening bid of one club is made on weaker hands that contain no five-card suit other than clubs.

Since every change of suit is forcing in the New South Wales system, there is no need for a forcing jump shift. Single jumps in a new suit are thus available for use as low-level asking bids.

The last bid in each of the above sequences is an asking bid agreeing partner's suit as trumps. There are obvious advantages in being able to start an asking sequence at such a low level. The extra round of bidding space that is created can make all the difference when it comes to discovering the last vital control needed for a slam.

The main feature of the Australian responses to asking bids is the distinction made between the king and a singleton in the asked suit when two outside aces are held. With the king in the asked suit the normal no trump response is made. With a singleton the responder jumps in the suit of his cheaper ace (but not in trumps, of course).

Here is an example of this response from the "test match" between Australia and a visiting American team in early 1970.

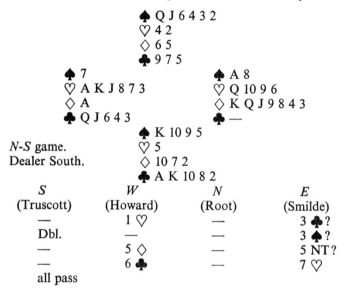

♠ Q J 6 4 3 2
♡ 4 2
◇ 6 5
♣ 9 7 5

♠ 7   ♠ A 8
♡ A K J 8 7 3   ♡ Q 10 9 6
◇ A   ◇ K Q J 9 8 4 3
♣ Q J 6 4 3   ♣ —

♠ K 10 9 5
N-S game.   ♡ 5
Dealer South.   ◇ 10 7 2
       ♣ A K 10 8 2

S	W	N	E
(Truscott)	(Howard)	(Root)	(Smilde)
—	1 ♡	—	3 ♣?
Dbl.	—	—	3 ♠?
—	5 ◇	—	5 NT?
—	6 ♣	—	7 ♡
all pass			

By passing the double of three clubs West denied a club control. That was good news, and East asked again in spades, learning that his partner had a singleton spade and the aces of hearts and diamonds. The six-club response to the TAB of 5 NT showed (at that time) the king of trumps, which enabled East to bid the grand slam.

It is only fair to mention that in the other room the American pair, Jordan and Robinson, had no trouble in bidding the grand slam without the aid of asking bids.

On that hand, as it happened, it made no difference whether West held the king of spades or a singleton, but one can easily imagine hands on which it is vital to distinguish between the two holdings.

K

♠ A	♠ J 9 6	W	E
♡ K Q 8 7 5 3	♡ A 9 4	1 ♡	2 ♣
◇ A Q J 4 3	◇ K 6	2 ◇	3 ♡
♣ 7	♣ A J 8 5 4	4 ◇?	4 NT
		7 ♡	—

The change of suit by the opener is forcing to game, and the jump preference shows slam interest. After asking in diamonds and hearing a no trump response, West is fortified by the knowledge that his partner is promising the king and not just a singleton in diamonds.

There are two other differences in the Australian responses to asking bids. A jump in the asked suit is used to show a void in the asked suit with two aces, and a double jump in trumps to show a void in the asked suit and three aces. Since these responses are space-consuming, it is just as well that it is possible to begin asking at a low level.

How would you like to be able to use a bid of two no trumps as a TAB? The Australians can do it in certain sequences. Once a major suit has been agreed as trumps, a no trump bid at the cheapest level is a TAB.

W	E		W	E
1 ♠	2 ♣		1 ◇	1 ♡
2 ◇	2 ♠		3 ♡	3 NT?
2 NT?				

In each case the last bid queries the trump holding.

Since the ace of trumps can always be shown at a later (or earlier) stage in response to a suit asking bid, the Australian TAB is concerned primarily with the king and queen of trumps. Lacking both the king and the queen, the responder signs off in the trump suit. The other responses are by steps, the trump suit not counting as a step. Here is the current schedule.

1st step — queen.
2nd step — king.
3rd step — king and one extra trump.
4th step — king and queen.
5th step — king and queen and one extra trump.

By an extra trump is meant one more than the minimum number guaranteed by the responder's previous bidding.

Repeat Asking Bids

The Australians do not go along with the South African modifications regarding repeat asking bids. They stick fairly closely to the original Culbertson method, using the repeat ask after a negative response to query third-round control and outside aces as well as second-round control without aces.

The repeat ask after a positive response showing two or three aces is used as a request for clarification of the aces held. The responses to this repeat ask are:

1. When the response to the original asking bid was a minimum no trump bid,

(*a*) Without the ace of the asked suit—bid trumps.

(*b*) With the ace in the asked suit—bid the other ace suit (or no trumps if the other ace is in trumps).

2. When the response to the original asking bid was a jump in the lower ace suit—bid the other ace suit.

3. When the response to the original asking bid showed three aces by a jump in no trumps—bid the suit in which the ace is missing.

This method comes into its own when the asker has a void in his hand.

♠ K 10 9 6 5 3	♠ A 8 4 2	*W*	*E*
♡ —	♡ K 9 8 4	1 ♠	3 ♠
♢ Q 7 4	♢ A K 6 3	4 ♢ ?	4 NT
♣ A K Q 8	♣ 6	5 ♢ ?	5 NT
		6 ♢ ?	6 ♡
		7 ♠	—

In the New South Wales system the double raise is forcing and suggestive of slam. The response to the repeat ask in diamonds tells West that his partner holds the right aces, and there is still room to check up on second-round diamond control.

ROME

In the Roman Club system, developed by Walter Avarelli and Giorgio Belladonna and played by them with outstanding success in many World Championships, asking bids of a very different nature are used. The divergence from the Culbertson method is two-fold. Roman asking bids enquire about controls in one suit at a time, and the responses are made on the step principle.

The Roman Club is a distributional bidding system, and many of its unique conventions have been adopted by keen tournament players all over the world. The asking bids are no exception. They fit easily into the framework of any other system, and have in part been incorporated into Kaplan-Sheinwold methods.

One or two modifications have been introduced in recent years, but it is open to question whether these represent a significant improvement. In this chapter we shall examine the original version, which is still the more widely used.

Regular Asking Bids

The asking bids concerned with controls are defined as regular. They are normally made by a jump bid which agrees trumps implicitly, but after direct trump agreement at the three-level or higher the bid of a new suit without a jump may be an asking bid.

W	E		W	E		W	E
1 ♡	2 ♡		1 ♡	3 ♡		1 ♠	4 ♠
3 ♠ ?			3 ♠ ?			5 ♣ ?	
W	E		W	E		W	E
2 ♠	4 ♡ ?		2 ♡	4 ◇ ?		1 ♠	2 ♣
						2 ♡	4 ◇ ?

In each sequence the last bid queries partner's controls in the suit. The conventional step responses (designated Type Alpha) are as follows:

> 1st step — no control
> 2nd step — king or singleton
> 3rd step — ace or void
> 4th step — AK or AQ

If the opponents interfere over an asking bid, the pass becomes the first step, and next higher suit the second step and so on.

While the information obtained by these asking bids is limited to the one suit, the method has the virtue of simplicity. Here are some examples.

♠ 9 3	♠ A 8 6	W	E
♡ K 9 8 3	♡ A Q 7 5 4	1 ♡	3 ♡
◇ A K Q 6 5 2	◇ 4	3 ♠?	4 ◇
♣ A	♣ J 8 5 3	7 ♡	—

In the *canapé* style of the Roman Club system one heart is the opening bid on the West hand. The response of three hearts shows 10–14 points and five-card trump support including two of the three top honours. When West asks in spades the three-step response assures him that his partner holds the ace or a void, which is all he needs to know.

♠ A K 10 7 4 3	♠ Q J 8 5	W	E
♡ 6 4	♡ A K Q 9	2 ♠	4 ◇?
◇ 6	◇ 9 7 3	4 ♠	4 NT?
♣ A 9 8 3	♣ K 5	5 ♡	6 ♠

The opening bid of two spades shows five or more spades and four or more clubs. East asks immediately in diamonds, learns about second-round control, and bids the slam after checking on aces via Roman Blackwood.

A further type of regular asking bid involves an immediate jump shift in response to an opening bid of one in a suit.

W	E	W	E	W	E
1 ♠	3 ♣?	1 ♡	3 ◇?	1 ◇	3 ♡?

Note that in order to ask in the next higher suit, as in the last sequence, a double jump is required. This is because one heart is the negative step response to one diamond, hence a jump to two hearts would merely indicate positive values with a good heart suit.

After the above sequences the responses are varied so as to differentiate between aces and voids, kings and singletons.

1st step	— no control
2nd step	— singleton
3rd step	— void
4th step	— king
5th step	— ace

Here is an example of the immediate jump shift.

♠ K Q 9 6	♠ A 10 8 7 4	*W*	*E*
♡ K Q J 8 3	♡ —	1 ♠	3 ♣ ?
◇ 7 5	◇ A 8	3 NT	5 NT ?
♣ K 5	♣ A Q J 6 3 2	7 ♠	—

East asks at once in clubs in order to find out if his partner has a vital control in the suit. When West admits to the king by giving a four-step response, all that East need do is apply the grand slam force.

The responses to the TAB of 5 NT, which is always a jump in Roman methods, are as follows:

> No top honour — six clubs
> One — six of trump suit
> Two — seven of trump suit.

Special Asking Bids

In the Roman system the opening bid of one club normally denotes a balanced hand. Occasionally, however, the bid is made on strong unbalanced hands containing no more than four losers. It is after this type of one club opening that the special asking bids come into play. The opener, who does the asking, is concerned not so much with controls as with the degree of support held by his partner for his long suit. He asks by jumping the bidding on the second round.

W	*E*		*W*	*E*		*W*	*E*
1 ♣	1 ◇		1 ♣	1 ♠		1 ♣	1 ◇
2 ♡ ?			3 ♡ ?			2 ◇ ?	

After a negative response of one diamond, the opener does not need to jump to ask in a minor suit, for the rebids of two clubs and two diamonds are not used after one club has been opened on a balanced hand.

The conventional responses to this special asking bid, (designated Type Beta), are in nine steps as follows:

> 1st step — singleton or void
> 2nd step — two or three small cards
> 3rd step — ace, king or queen singleton

4th step — a top honour with one or two small cards
5th step — four small cards
6th step — four or more cards including a top honour
7th step — two top honours
8th step — four or more cards with two top honours
9th step — three top honours

If an opponent intervenes over the asking bid, the responder makes his normal response if able to do so. If his response has been crowded out, he passes. The opener can ask again by doubling, whereupon the steps start afresh from the opponent's bid.

After the response to one of these special asking bids the opener can ask the same question about another suit without a further jump. He will continue to receive Type Beta responses as long as his asking bids are made in ascending order. A further asking bid made in descending order is for controls, requiring a Type Alpha response.

The chain of asking bids is broken when the opener bids no trumps, repeats a suit, or makes a game bid after a discouraging response.

The nine-step responses may seem complicated, but the special asking bids play a vital role in identifying trump support for slam purposes. Here is an example.

♠ A Q 9 6 3	♠ K 8 7 2	*W*	*E*
♡ A K	♡ Q 7 5 4	1 ♣	1 ♡
◇ A K 10 6 5	◇ 9	3 ◇?	3 ♡
♣ 7	♣ K 10 6 3	3 ♠?	4 NT
		5 ♣?	5 ♡
		6 ♠	—

The positive response of one heart shows upwards of seven points and at least four hearts. West jumps to three diamonds to ask about support, and the first-step response shows a singleton or void. West asks again in spades, still for support since it is in ascending order, and hears a six-step response promising four cards including a top honour. The club ask is for controls since it is made in descending order. The two-step Type Alpha response indicates the king, and West has to be content with a small slam.

Note that West had to plan the bidding carefully, asking first in diamonds so that he could investigate support for both suits. If West had bid two spades on the second round and found his partner without support, he would have been left with no way of checking the diamond fit.

A second type of special asking bid is used after a positive response to an opening bid of one club. A jump raise by the opener queries his partner's honour holding in the suit. The responses (designated Type Gamma) are as follows:

1st step — queen or less
2nd step — king
3rd step — ace
4th step — two top honours
5th step — three top honours

This low-level TAB investigates the solidity of the trump suit for either small or grand slam purposes.

The four-step Type Gamma response satisfies West about the trump position and leaves him free to check on the ace of hearts. If West had asked first in hearts he would have left himself without a means of checking on the solidity of the spades.

CHINA

The most interesting development of recent years has been the meteoric rise of the Precision Club system, the brain-child of New York shipping magnate Charles C. Wei. Playing Precision under the captaincy of Mr. Wei, the Nationalist Chinese team reached the final of the World Championship in both 1969 and 1970 and has never been far from the top in subsequent international events. Precision players have also had notable success in the United States, winning both of the premier team trophies, the Spingold (twice) and the Vanderbilt.

Precision is by far the simplest of all the big club systems, and this largely accounts for its growing popularity. Based on an artificial opening bid of one club for almost all hands of 16 points or more, a weak no trump and five-card majors, the system is easy to use and guides its players to the right denomination at the right level with remarkable frequency.

In the slam zone Precision makes use of a number of asking bids which, while similar in style to the Roman variety, have interesting features of their own.

Trump Asking Bid

This comes into play at a low level, after an opening bid of one club and a positive response in a suit. A simple raise by the opener asks for definition of trump length and strength. The conventional step responses are as follows:

1st step — no top honour
2nd step — five cards with one top honour
3rd step — five cards with two top honours
4th step — six cards with one top honour
5th step — six cards with two top honours
6th step — three top honours

As always, the low-level TAB avoids problems on those hands where a grand slam force might take the bidding too high.

♠ Q 8 6 4	♠ J 10 7 5 2	*W*	*E*
♡ A K 6	♡ Q 8 3	1 ♣	1 ♠
◇ A K Q 8 7 3	◇ 6	2 ♠?	2 NT
♣ —	♣ A Q 10 5	4 ♠	—

The one-step response to the TAB of two spades tells West that the top trumps are missing.

It might be thought that this treatment could lead to embarrassment when the opener has no slam ambitions and merely wishes to show support for his partner's suit. The opener can deal with this situation quite simply, however, by choosing one no trump as his first rebid and supporting his partner on the next round.

Control Asking Bids

After a TAB, or at any time when trumps have been agreed, the bid of a new suit is an enquiry for controls. The responder indicates his holding in the suit as follows:

1st step   — no control
2nd step   — queen or doubleton
3rd step   — king or singleton
4th step   — ace or void
5th step   — AK or AQ

The difference from the Roman schedule lies in the admission of third-round controls. This can be very useful.

♠ A K	♠ J 7 3	W	E
♡ A K 10 9 3	♡ 7 4	1 ♣	2 ♣
◇ 5	◇ A 10 6	3 ♣?	3 ♠
♣ K 9 8 6 2	♣ A Q 10 5 4	4 ◇?	5 ♣
		5 ♡?	5 NT
		7 ♣	—

The three-step response to the TAB shows five clubs headed by the ace and queen, the response to the diamond ask indicates the ace or a void, and the response to the heart ask shows third-round control to complete the picture.

A repeat asking bid requests clarification of the previous response. This time the responder has only two steps to choose between.

1st step   — control by shortage
2nd step   — control by high card

This caters for the situations where the asker needs a high card in the suit rather than a singleton or void.

♠ A K Q 7 6 2	♠ J 10 4	W	E
♡ —	♡ J 10 7 5 4	1 ♣	1 ◇
◇ A Q J 3 2	◇ K 6	2 ♠	3 ♠
♣ A K	♣ 8 7 5	4 ◇?	4 NT
		5 ◇?	5 ♠
		7 ♠	—

The repeat ask in diamonds is used to discover whether East has the king or a singleton. If East had shown a singleton diamond West would have bid six spades only, taking the view that there would be too much work to do in a grand slam.

Ace Asking Bids

In most sequences a jump shift in a forcing situation asks for aces and also queries top cards in the asked suit. The responses this time do not follow the step principle.

Holding in asked suit	Holding elsewhere	Action
No top honour	No ace	Bid no trumps
,, ,,	1 ace	Bid ace suit
,, ,,	2 aces	Jump in no trumps
Top honour	No ace	Raise asked suit
,, ,,	1 ace	Jump in ace suit
,, ,,	2 aces	Jump raise asked suit

This asking bid can be particularly useful when the opener has a strong hand with a near-solid suit.

♠ A K	♠ J 9 4	W E
♡ K Q J 9	♡ A 6 3	1 ♣ 2 ♣
◇ A K J 9 7 5 4	◇ Q	3 ◇ ? 4 ♡
♣ —	♣ K Q 8 7 4 3	7 ◇ —

West hears about the queen of diamonds and the ace of hearts in the one response.

Like the Roman variety, Precision asking bids are adaptable and can easily be grafted on to any other system.

10 · When Clubs are Blue

In the slam zone the Blue Club system depends largely on a comprehensive style of cue-bidding that is worthy of special study. The Blue Club is the final distillation of the Neapolitan system, designed by Professor Eugenio Chiaradia and used with enormous success by Benito Garozzo and Pietro Forquet in defending a dozen world titles with Italy's Blue Team. Other players also contributed to the development of the Blue Club, notably Leon Yallouze and Claude Delmouly who, along with Garozzo, Forquet and Belladonna, toured with Omar Sharif's Bridge Circus, bringing great publicity to the system and to bridge in general.

Basically, Blue Club is a big club system featuring control-showing responses. Most hands containing 17 or more points are opened with a bid of one club. Exceptions are balanced hands of 21-22 points which are opened with a bid of two no trumps, and hands with 17-24 points and 4-4-4-1 distribution which are opened with a bid of two diamonds. Opening bids of one of a suit other than clubs show less than 17 points and are natural in the *canapé* style. The opening bid of one no trump has a wide range of 13-17 points, but the machinery available to the responder is such that no accuracy is lost. The opening bid of two clubs shows a good club suit with less than 17 points, while two hearts and two spades are weak opening bids.

The Blue Club is designed to enable a disciplined pair to achieve a high degree of accuracy at all levels, but it is in the slam zone that the precision of the system is most marked. The distinctive feature of the Blue Club cue-bidding style is that first-round and second-round controls are treated alike in the first instance. A player starts a cue-bidding sequence by bidding his cheapest control, whether it be an ace, king, singleton or void. His partner responds in like manner by bidding *his* cheapest control, and the exchange of cue-bids continues in economical fashion until either a sign-off bid is passed or a slam is reached. Bidding economy is enhanced by the frequent use of 4 NT and 5 NT as general cue-bids.

A bid of 4 NT can, in fact, have three distinct interpretations.

1. Blackwood

4 NT is treated as Blackwood in two situations.
(a) When it occurs on the first or second round of bidding.
(b) When it is a jump bid.

2. Quantitative

In certain obvious situations a bid of 4 NT may be a quantitative no trump raise, asking partner to bid six if he has a little extra.

3. General Slam Try

When it occurs in the middle of a series of cue-bids, 4 NT is interpreted as a general slam try. It enables a player with all-round values to mark time while awaiting a further cue-bid from his partner.

Similarly, a bid of 5 NT can have three different meanings.

1. Blackwood

5 NT asks for kings only when it follows a Blackwood bid of 4 NT.

2. Grand Slam Force

A jump to 5 NT is the grand slam force asking about top honours in trumps. Blue Club uses a comprehensive scale of responses, assigning a meaning to every six-level bid below the level of trumps.

When the jump to 5 NT is not available, the Baron slam try is used to query the trump holding.

3. General Slam Try

In all other cases the bid of 5 NT is a general grand slam try, normally confirming possession of all first-round controls and asking partner to show an additional feature if he can.

Let us study the logic of the Blue Club style with the aid of a few example hands.

♠ A K 10 8 7 3	♠ Q 9 5 4	W	E
♡ 5	♡ A Q 9 2	1 ♠	3 ♠
◇ A Q 6	◇ K 7 2	4 ◇	4 ♠
♣ Q 6 3	♣ 8 7	—	

Using orthodox methods East would certainly cue-bid his ace of hearts on the second round. Playing Blue Club cue-bids, however, he is not permitted to do this. By making his first cue-bid in diamonds West denies both first-round and second-round control of clubs, and East knows immediately that no slam is on. It is his duty to make this clear to his partner by signing off in four spades irrespective of his controls elsewhere.

A cue-bid of four hearts by East in this situation would affirm control of clubs as well as hearts.

♠ A K 10 8 7 3	♠ Q 9 5 4	W	E
♡ 5	♡ A J 9 2	1 ♠	3 ♠
◇ A Q 6	◇ K 7 3 2	4 ◇	4 ♡
♣ Q 6 3	♣ 8	4 ♠	5 ◇
		6 ♠	—

With the above hand East is free to cue-bid his ace of hearts since he possesses control of clubs as well. West can do no more for the moment, but East properly considers his controls in three suits to be worth a further effort. Note that he bids five diamonds and not five clubs, however. He has already shown the club control by inference. To "repeat" this by bidding five clubs would, in fact, promise the ace.

West can now be sure that his partner has second-round control in both minor suits plus the ace of hearts, for East would not have advanced to the five-level without an ace in his hand. The value of the Blue Club method lies in the abundance of inferences, both positive and negative, that arise in a simple cue-bidding sequence.

Let us try a further variation on the East hand.

		W	E
♠ A K 10 8 7 3	♠ Q 9 5 4	1 ♠	3 ♠
♡ 5	♡ 10 9 6 2	4 ◇	5 ♣
◇ A Q 6	◇ 7	5 ♡	6 ♠
♣ Q 6 3	♣ A K J 8		

This time East is in a position to reassure his partner about the club suit, at the same time denying a heart control by skipping the suit. West promises that the hearts are under control, whereupon East bids the slam.

		W	E
♠ A J 6 3	♠ K 10 9 7 4 2	2 ♣	2 ♠
♡ 9 4	♡ 5	4 ◇	4 ♡
◇ 2	◇ A J 8 3	6 ♠	—
♣ A K Q 7 6 5	♣ 8 4		

The two-club opening bid shows a good club suit with less than 17 points, and the response of two spades is not forcing. The jump to four diamonds is one of the special bids used in Blue Club to indicate a big trump fit. As well as showing excellent spade support it promises a diamond control. East reciprocates by showing his heart control, thus enabling West to bid the slam.

In general a responsive cue-bid below game level does not indicate extra values and may show either first-round or second-round control. When his partner is limited, however, a player is obviously expected to use his discretion in deciding whether or not to make a cue-bid. In the last example, for instance, if East held the king and queen of diamonds instead of the ace it would not be sensible for him to show his heart control. On hearing the responsive cue-bid West is entitled to assume that his partner has an ace in one of the red suits.

In Blue Club slam-bidding methods the jump to indicate a super-fit plays an important role by conveying precise information about controls. The next hand illustrates this point and also features the general cue-bid of four no trumps.

♠ A K 10 6 5	♠ Q J 8 2	W	E
♥ K 8	♥ A 9 4	1 ◇	1 ♠
◇ A J 10 7 5	◇ K	4 ◇	4 ♡
♣ 3	♣ A Q 7 6 4	4 ♠	4 NT
		5 ♣	5 ◇
		5 ♡	6 ♡
		7 ♠	—

West's second-round jump to four diamonds indicates a strong (15-16 point) two-suiter, with spades at least as long as diamonds. The jump also shows first-round control of diamonds and denies first-round control of clubs. East cue-bids his heart control and West, who has pretty well shown his hand, signs off in four spades.

But East has not finished by a long way. At this point he might bid five clubs himself, but rightly prefers four no trumps because he wishes to hear if his partner has club control. The bid of four no trumps has the effect of rectifying the timing of the cue-bidding sequence and permitting all second-round controls to be shown at the five-level.

There can be no mistaking the meaning of East's final effort of six hearts. If East needed to hear about extra values in the side suits he had bids of 5 NT, six clubs or six diamonds available to him. Six hearts is clearly a grand slam force, therefore, asking West to bid seven if he holds two of the three top honours in trumps.

When a player by-passes an unbid side-suit in going to four no trumps, he clearly denies control in that suit.

♠ K 6	♠ 9 5	W	E
♥ K J 4 3	♥ A Q 10 7 5	1 ♡	2 ♣
◇ A Q 9 6 2	◇ K 3	2 ◇	4 ♣
♣ 7 4	♣ A K Q 3	4 ◇	4 NT
		6 ♡	—

The second-round jump to four clubs shows a big fit in hearts. West cue-bids his diamond ace and East by-passes spades in bidding four no trumps. This shows a very powerful hand and conveys the message that spade control is all that is needed for the slam.

Precise information about point-count and distribution can be obtained after an opening bid of one no trump.

♠ A 6 4	♠ K 9 3	W	E
♡ K 7	♡ A Q 6 2	1 NT	2 ◇
◇ A Q 7 6	◇ K J 10 3	3 ♣	3 ◇
♣ K 9 5 2	♣ A 8	3 NT	4 ◇
		4 ♡	4 ♠
		5 ♣	5 ♡
		5 ♠	6 ♣
		7 ◇	—

The conventional response of two diamonds forces to game, and the rebid of three clubs shows 16-17 points with no major suit. The relay of three diamonds asks about minor suits, three no trumps shows four cards in each, and four diamonds indicates slam interest in the suit.

A series of cue-bids follows, and by the time East hears five spades from his partner he knows that there are no losers outside the trump suit. The TAB of six clubs asks the final question, and West bids the grand slam on the strength of his two top honours.

When the auction starts with a bid of one club, the opener normally learns on the first round the precise number of controls held by his partner. Counting a king as one control and an ace as two, the responder bids as follows:

1 ◇ — 0-2 controls and less than 6 points
1 ♡ — 0-2 controls and 6 or more points
1 ♠ — 3 controls (AK or KKK)
1 NT— 4 controls
2 ♣ — 5 controls
2 ◇ — 6 controls
2 NT— 7 controls

The responses of two hearts and two spades are natural and weak, showing a six-card suit with two honour cards but less than six points.

For slam purposes the opener may need to know not only the number but the location of his partner's controls. After trump agreement the responder is expected to show where his controls lie in so far as he can do so below game level. He should not make a cue-bid above game level unless invited to do so by a strong bid from the opener.

♠ A Q J 4	♠ K 7 3	W	E
♡ K Q 9 6 5 4	♡ A 8 7	1 ♣	1 ♠
◇ A K Q	◇ 9 6 5	2 ♡	3 ♡
♣ —	♣ J 8 6 5	3 ♠	4 ♡
		7 ♡	—

The response of one spade shows three controls, which West knows in this case must be an ace and a king. When East fails to cue-bid in clubs on the third round West realises that his partner must hold the ace of hearts and the king of spades—just the cards he needs.

In Blue Club methods it is often possible to locate third-round controls.

♠ 7	♠ A K 9 4	W	E
♡ A 6	♡ 9 4 3	1 ♣	2
◇ K Q J 8 6 5	◇ A 7 3 2	2 ◇	3 ◇
♣ A K 5 3	♣ 8 6	3 ♡	3
		4 ♣	4
		5 ♣	5 ◇
		5 NT	6
		7 ◇	—

The response of two clubs shows five controls, and West realises at once that his partner's club holding is the key to the grand slam. He has no real interest in locating his partner's major suit king, but after trump agreement he goes through the motions of a disciplined cue-bidding sequence, building up to the point where he can use the general cue-bid of five no trumps to ask his partner for an undisclosed feature. With a doubleton club and adequate trumps, East makes the bid that his partner wants to hear.

♠ A Q J 9 7 4	♠ K 6	W	E
♡ K 8 3	♡ A 5 4	1 ♣	1 NT
◇ A 6	◇ 10 9 3	2 ♠	3
♣ A 4	♣ K Q 8 7 2	3 ♠	4
		4 NT	5
		5 ◇	5 ♡
		5 NT	6
		7 ♣	—

The response of one no trump indicates four controls, and

after trump agreement West gives his partner every opportunity to disclose where these controls lie. When West bids five no trumps he is still not sure whether the king of spades is missing or not, but East's bid of six clubs completes the picture. Holding the king of diamonds East would bid six diamonds at this point. The bid of six clubs affirms possession of the queen of clubs and also the king of spades, making it safe for West to bid the grand slam.

After an opening bid of one club there is little risk of landing in a grand slam missing an ace or a small slam lacking two aces. But after other opening bids this danger is ever present owing to the inherent ambiguity of a cue-bidding style that treats aces, kings, singletons and voids as equals. The problem can sometimes be overcome by repeating a cue-bid at a high level to guarantee first-round control in the suit.

♠ 7	♠ A 8 3	W	E
♡ K 9 4	♡ A Q J 10 6 5	1 ◇	2 ♡
◇ A J 6 5 2	◇ K Q	3 ♡	3 ♠
♣ A 9 6 3	♣ 8 4	4 ♣	4 ◇
		4 ♠	4 NT
		5 ◇	5 NT
		6 ♣	7 ♡

The jump shift guarantees a suit with no more than one loser and the raise promises an honour card, so both partners know at an early stage that the trumps are solid. The usual careful series of cue-bids follows, and by the fifth round the only question worrying East is whether his partner has first-round or second-round control of clubs. He marks time with the general slam try of five no trumps, and West takes the opportunity to affirm first-round club control by repeating the cue-bid.

These examples should give some idea of what the Blue Club cue-bidding style is all about. The auctions may appear to be long-winded but they are remarkably thorough. The economy of the style makes it possible on most hands to discover every vital feature and to place the final contract with great accuracy.

The judgement of each player is subjected to heavy pressure, however, and to my mind this is a major defect of the method. Where are the players capable of conducting long dialogues with patience and discipline, picking up every subtle inference and guiding the auction to its logical conclusion without once sounding a false note?

Although full of admiration for the ingenuity of the method, I doubt if there are many players capable of handling it. Blue Club cue-bids are designed for super-men. Players whose judgement is not consistently good are likely to find the method accident-prone.

Even the super-men have problems. Here is the first hand played on bridgerama in the rubber bridge challenge match between the Omar Sharif Circus and Flint—Cansino.

♠ 5	♠ A K J 9 7	*W*	*E*
♡ A Q 8 7 5	♡ K J 9 4	(Sharif)	(Delmouly)
◇ A K 7	◇ Q 9 4	1 ♣	1 NT
♣ A Q 8 3	♣ 6	2 ♡	3 ♡
		4 ♣	4 ♠
		4 NT	5 ♣
		5 ◇	5 ♠
		6 ♡	—

At £1 per point, missing the grand slam cost the Circus a cool £500. Sharif was apparently convinced that his partner had categorically denied holding the king of hearts on the above sequence. Was Delmouly right to show his singleton club before indicating where his remaining high cards lay? If so, Sharif should surely have introduced a TAB.

The lesson of the deal is that close partnership understanding as well as excellent judgement is needed in order to succeed with Blue Club methods. This was not by any means the only misunderstanding in the match. There were several more serious disasters, including a grand slam lacking an ace bid by Belladonna and Sharif and a small slam with two aces missing bid by Garozzo and Belladonna.

It is a matter of record that the Blue-Clubbers won the marathon match by 5470 points, but they did not win it on the strength of their slam bidding.

By all means try out the Blue Club cue-bids, for the education of a tournament player cannot be complete without some experience of the beauty and subtlety of this style. But do not expect instant success. You must be prepared to travel a rocky road and suffer a number of setbacks before achieving any expertise with the method.

Blue Club Two Diamonds

The Roman idea of using an opening bid of two diamonds to denote a strong three-suited hand has been adopted with enthusiasm by players in many parts of the world. The Blue Club version limits the bids to hand of 4-4-4-1 distribution in the 17-24 point range.

Such hands may not turn up very often, but the accuracy of the Blue Club in dealing with them is such that I believe the method to be well worth incorporating in any two-club system.

In its approach to slam bidding after an opening bid of two diamonds the Blue Club style undergoes a radical change. The equal rights enjoyed by both partners in the cue-bidding exchanges are replaced by a master and slave relationship. After opening with a bid of two diamonds and hearing the normal two heart response, the opener is restricted to making codified conventional bids while the responder milks him dry of information about his strength and shape. This is not an ideal relationship between partners, but it is undeniably effective on these hands and tolerable enough in small doses.

Here is a summary of the Blue Club method.

Responses to 2 ◇

There are four possible responses—2 ♡, 2 ♠, 2 NT and three of a suit. We shall consider each of these in turn.

2 ♡ Response

This is the normal conventional relay response used on nine hands out of ten. It shows neither strength nor weakness, merely asking the opener to clarify his holding. The other three responses are made on specialised hands.

2 ♠ Response

This is a natural negative response, showing four or more spades and less than six points. The response may have to be made with only three spades when the hand contains only one four-card suit.

2 NT Response

This is semi-positive (6 or 7 points), showing a six-card suit headed by two honour cards one of which is the ace or king.

Response of 3 ♣, 3 ♢, 3 ♡ or 3 ♠

These responses show weaker six-card suits headed by the ace, king or queen-knave.

The specialised responses rarely lead to slam contracts, and we shall look only briefly at the developments after these responses before moving on to consider the more interesting response of two hearts.

Developments after 2 ♢-2 ♠

With a hand in the weaker half of the range (17-20) the opener passes with a spade fit and bids 2 NT with a singleton spade.

With a hand in the stronger half of the range (21-24) the opener bids the suit below his singleton.

> 3 ♣ with a singleton diamond
> 3 ♢ with a singleton heart
> 3 ♡ with a singleton spade
> 3 ♠ with a singleton club

The responder either passes or makes the final bid.

♠ A K Q 3	♠ J 9 4	W	E
♡ A Q J 6	♡ 8 7 5 2	2 ♢	2 ♠
♢ 5	♢ 9 4 2	3 ♣	4 ♡
♣ A J 7 3	♣ Q 10 5		

East does not have much, but his hand is improved by the knowledge that his partner has a singleton diamond.

Developments after 2 ♢-2 NT

Irrespective of his strength the opener rebids in the suit below his singleton. The responder then bids his suit, and if this coincides with the singleton the opener passes with 17-20 and bids 3 NT with 21-24.

An exceptional case arises when the bidding starts 2 ◇-2 NT, 3 ♠. In order not to by-pass the no trump game the responder must bid 3 NT if his suit is clubs. Opener then passes with 21-24 and takes out into 4 ♣ with 17-20.

When a fit is revealed by the responder's second bid the opener either goes straight to game or cue-bids at the cheapest level. In the latter event the responder is expected to show any singleton he possesses.

		W	E
A J 7 6	♠ 3	2 ◇	2 NT
♡ A K Q 4	♡ 10 6 5	3 ♠	4 ◇
◇ K 9 8 4	◇ A J 7 6 3 2	4 ♡	4 ♠
♣ 7	♣ J 5 2	6 ◇	—

Developments after 2 ◇-3 ♣, etc.

When his singleton coincides with his partner's suit the opener passes with 17-20 and bids 3 NT with 21-24.

With a fit in his partner's suit the opener either raises to game or bids his singleton suit. This is the only occasion where the opener rebids in the singleton suit rather than the suit below. The responder rebids by steps to show his values.

1st step   — trumps headed by Q J.
2nd step — trumps headed by A or K but no singleton.
3rd step — trumps headed by A or K and a singleton.

The opener can cue-bid if he wishes to discover where the singleton lies.

		W	E
A	♠ Q J 3	2 ◇	3 ♡
♡ A 7 5 4	♡ K 9 8 6 3 2	3 ♠	4 ◇
◇ K Q J 6	◇ 9 4 3	4 ♠	5 ♣
♣ A 10 7 2	♣ 8	6 ♡	—

The three-step response of four diamonds shows the king of hearts plus an outside singleton, and West learns that it is the right singleton on the next round.

Developments after 2 ♢-2 ♡

Opener's rebids are codified all the way, and responder assumes complete responsibility for placing the contract.

Opener's first duty is to indicate his range and his singleton, which he does with the following rebids:

2 ♠ — 17-20, major suit singleton.
2 NT—   ,,   club   ,,
3 ♣ —   ,,   diamond   ,,
3 ♢ — 21-24, heart   ,,
3 ♡ —   ,,   spade   ,,
3 ♠ —   ,,   club   ,,
3 NT—   ,,   diamond   ,,

The 2 ♠ rebid is the only one that does not immediately define the singleton. The responder makes a relay bid of 2 NT to enquire whether a singleton spade or heart is held and to ask for a closer definition of the range.

After 2 ♢-2 ♡, 2 ♠-2 NT:

3 ♣ — shows a singleton heart.
3 ♢ — shows a singleton spade and 17-18 points.
3 ♡ — shows a singleton spade and 19-20 points.

When the opener shows a singleton heart, the responder can make a further relay bid in hearts to ask about the range. After 2 ♢-2 ♡, 2 ♠-2 NT, 3 ♣-3 ♡:

3 ♠ — shows 17-18.
3 NT— shows 19-20.

When the opener has shown 17-20 points with a singleton club or diamond, the responder can again bid the short suit to ask for a closer definition of range.

e.g.	W	E		W	E
	2 ♢	2 ♡		2 ♢	2 ♡
	2 NT	3 ♣		3 ♣	3 ♢
	3 ♢ — shows 17-18.			3 ♡ — shows 17-18.	
	3 ♡ — shows 19-20.			3 ♠ — shows 19-20.	

At this point any bid by the responder, apart from a further relay in the short suit, terminates the auction. The only exception is that a bid of four in a minor suit invites the opener to continue to five if he has two honour cards in the suit.

Let us see some examples.

♠ 6	♠ 7 5 4	W	E
♡ A K 7 3	♡ J 8 6 4	2 ◇	2 ♡
◇ A K 4 2	◇ Q 8 7 5	2 ♠	2 NT
♣ K Q 9 3	♣ 5 2	3 ♡	4 ♡

When East hears that his partner has 19-20 points with a singleton spade he judges game to be worth bidding. If on the third round West had bid three diamonds to show 17-18 points, East would have closed the bidding at three hearts.

♠ A K Q 2	♠ 8 5	W	E
♡ K J 9 4	♡ 6 5	2 ◇	2 ♡
◇ 7	◇ Q 9 6 4 3	3 ♣	—
♣ A 8 7 2	♣ Q 9 5 3		

East has no reason to bid again.

♠ A Q 7 3	♠ K J 6	W	E
♡ 4	♡ 10 8 7 2	2 ◇	2 ♡
◇ K J 4 2	◇ Q 8 6 5	2 ♠	2 NT
♣ A K J 5	♣ 7 4	3 ♣	3 ♡
		3 ♠	4 ◇
		5 ◇	—

After discovering his partner to have 17-18 points and a singleton heart, East invites game in diamonds. West accepts on the strength of his two honour cards in the suit.

Asking for Controls

When the opener's first rebid indicates a strong hand in the 21-24 point range, the responder does not attempt to obtain closer definition of the point-count. A relay bid in the short suit now asks for controls, as does a further relay by a responder who has already learned about the exact point-range of a 17-20 opener. The responder should, of course, see some prospect of slam before he enquires about controls.

Counting an ace as two controls and a king as one, the opener bids by steps to show the number of controls he holds. The steps show from four to eight controls in the 17-20 zone and from six to ten in the 21-24 zone.

e.g.	W	E			W	E	
	2 ◇	2 ♡			2 ◇	2 ♡	
	2 ♠	2 NT			3 ♡	3 ♠	
	3 ♣	3 ♡			3 NT—shows six controls		
	3 NT	4 ♡			4 ♣	—	seven
	4 ♠	—shows four controls			4 ◇	—	eight
	4 NT—		five		4 ♡	—	nine
	5 ♣	—	six		4 ♠	—	ten
	5 ◇	—	seven				
	5 ♡	—	eight				

The number of controls shown by the opener will often enable the responder to identify the holding precisely.

♠ A Q J 7	♠ K 6	W	E
♡ A K 6 5	♡ Q 9 8 4 2	2 ◇	2 ♡
◇ 5	◇ J 8 4	3 ♣	3 ◇
♣ A J 9 3	♣ K 4 2	3 ♠	4 ◇
		5 ♣	6 ♡

The seven controls shown by the opener can only be three aces and the king of hearts, and East knows that his partner must have at least one queen to make up his total of 19 points.

The responder does not need great strength to become slam-minded when his partner is in the 21-24 point zone.

♠ A K 9 3	♠ Q 7 6 5 2	W	E
♡ A K 5 4	♡ Q 8 6	2 ◇	2 ♡
◇ A K J 5	◇ 8	3 ♠	4 ♣
♣ 9	♣ J 8 4 3	4 NT	6 ♠

When the opener shows a singleton club and nine controls, his partner knows that the slam is good.

♠ A J 7 5	♠ K 3	W	E
♡ 6	♡ A 9 4	2 ◇	2 ♡
◇ A K J 8	◇ 10 7 6 5 4 2	3 ◇	3 ♡
♣ A K J 3	♣ 8 5	4 ♣	7 ◇

The opener's eight controls suffice to take care of all the losers in the responder's hand.

When his partner's controls do not quite fill all the gaps, the responder may make yet another relay bid in the short suit to ask for queens, but the wholesale showing of queens (first step for no queen, second step for one, etc.) will not always be helpful. In order to place the contract with accuracy the responder may need to know not just how many queens but *which* queens are held.

To overcome this problem I suggest the following method. After checking on controls the responder may ask about queens in the three known suits by bidding either the short suit or 4 NT, whichever is the cheaper. The opener springs to attention as follows:

With one queen	— he names the suit.
With two queens	— he bids the short suit.
With none or three	— he bids no trumps.

At first glance it may appear dangerous to bid no trumps (perhaps skipping several steps) with no queen, but in practice it is not so. The opener's strength is always known within a point or two, and the responder can have no reason to ask for queens if a negative response is both possible and embarrassing.

This is the sort of hand on which the responder needs to know which queen is held.

♠ 7	♠ 8 3 2	W	E
♡ A Q J 6	♡ K 10 9 4	2 ◇	2 ♡
◇ A K 9 2	◇ Q J	3 ♡	3 ♠
♣ A K 5 3	♣ J 10 8 6	4 ◇	4 ♠
		5 ♡	6 ♡

After learning that his partner has a singleton spade, 21-24 points and eight controls, East asks for queens by bidding four spades. When West promises the queen of hearts East bids the slam in that suit, secure in the knowledge that his club losers will be discarded on the diamonds. If West had shown the queen of clubs instead of the queen of hearts, East could have bid the slam in clubs with equal confidence. Clubs would also have been the safer trump suit if West had admitted to two queens.

A responder with grand slam aspirations will at times be worried about trump solidity. In the codified sequences that follow 2 ◇ no TAB is available since the opener is not permitted to know the trump suit until the bidding is over. Asking for specific queens will usually solve the problem, however.

♠ A 8 7 5	♠ K J 9 2	W	E
♡ 5	♡ A 8 6 3	2 ◇	2 ♡
◇ A Q 4 3	◇ K 7	2 ♠	2 NT
♣ A K 6 5	♣ Q J 9	3 ♣	3 ♡
		3 ♠	4 ♡
		5 ◇	5 ♡
		6 ◇	6 ♠

East learns that his partner has a singleton heart, 17-18 points and seven controls, and then asks for queens by bidding five hearts. When his partner shows the wrong queen he settles at the six-level. Naturally he would also have signed off in six if his partner had bid five no trumps to indicate no queen. But if West had been able to show the queen of spades a good grand slam would have been reached.

When the opener shows two queens, the responder may still be in doubt as to whether the queen of trumps is missing or not. In such cases a further relay in no trumps can be used to ask the opener to name the missing queen.

This refinement helps on hands like the following.

♠ A J 3 2	♠ K 8 6	W	E
♡ A K Q 7	♡ 5 2	2 ◇	2 ♡
◇ 9	◇ A 7 6	3 ♣	3 ◇
♣ Q J 9 7	♣ A K 8 6 4	3 ♡	4 ◇
		4 ♠	4 NT
		5 ◇	5 NT
		6 ♣	7 ♣

After hearing about the singleton diamond, 17-18 points and five controls, East uses 4 NT to check on queens. West admits to two queens, and the next bid of 5 NT asks which is missing. East can count thirteen tricks once he is assured that it is a major suit queen that is absent. He is in a position to pass a bid of six clubs, however, thus avoiding the grand slam when it is a dubious proposition.

That takes care of the queen position, but suppose it is the king of trumps that the responder is worried about. We can cater for this by stipulating that a bid of 5 NT by the responder, when not preceded by an enquiry for queens, asks the opener to name a missing king.

When the opener has two kings there are no complications.

♠ A K 7 4	♠ Q	W	E
♡ A J 8 6	♡ Q 7 3	2 ◇	2 ♡
◇ A	◇ J 4 2	3 ♣	3 ◇
♣ K J 4 3	♣ A 9 8 6 5 2	3 ♠	4 ◇
		5 ◇	5 NT
		6 ♡	7 ♣

The responder learns about the singleton diamond and 19-20 points. When he discovers that his partner has eight controls, East realises that the grand slam must be on ice unless it is the king of trumps that is missing. His bid of 5 NT queries the missing king, and West puts his mind at rest.

When the opener has only one king the position is not so simple, for he cannot afford to bid the king suit at the six-level. The solution is for the opener to bid the cheaper of the missing kings. If this is the trump suit the responder passes. Otherwise he converts to trumps, expecting the opener to pass without the king and bid the grand slam if he has it.

♠ A 7 6 4	♠ 2	W	E
♡ A K 9 2	♡ Q J 8 7 4 3	2 ◇	2 ♡
◇ A Q 8 6	◇ K 3	2 NT	3 ♣
♣ 3	♣ A 9 5 2	3 ◇	4 ♣
		4 NT	5 NT
		6 ◇	6 ♡
		7 ♡	—

The opener reveals a singleton club, 17-18 points and seven controls. Needing to know about the king of trumps, East asks with a bid of 5 NT. West denies the king of diamonds, whereupon East converts to the trump suit and leaves the rest to his partner.

The sequences that follow an opening bid of two diamonds are certainly complex and highly artificial, but if you examine them closely you will discover a logical basis for every manoeuvre.

In the long term it may be the Two Diamond convention rather than the cue-bidding style that proves to be the major contribution of the Blue Club system to slam-bidding technique.

11 · Two Clubs Modernised

For most players the forcing opening bid of two clubs still serves as one of the main launching platforms for slams. The Acol version of the bid has changed little since the system first came into being nearly forty years ago. The only modification to gain general acceptance has been a relaxation of the requirements for a positive response.

The old standard of an ace and a king, two king-queens, a king-queen and two kings, or four kings was found to be too restricting, and the modern tendency is to give a positive response on any hand containing either:

(*a*) An ace and a king.
(*b*) Eight points with one ace or two kings.
(*c*) Six or seven points including at least one king and a good five-card suit.

A positive response that involves going to the three-level in a minor suit should naturally promise rather more than the minimum specified in (*c*).

Jump Rebid by Opener

Traditionally a jump rebid by the opener indicates a solid suit and asks in the first instance for the responder to cue-bid any ace he holds.

The jump to three hearts sets the trump suit, and East is required to cue-bid an ace or sign off in three no trumps.

A refinement of this treatment, developed many years ago by

the Sharples brothers, is less well known than it deserves to be. This requires the responder to sign off with a blank hand by raising the opener's suit and to bid three no trumps only if his hand contains some feature that may be of interest for slam purposes.

After the three no trump response a bid of four clubs asks for kings. The responder cue-bids any king he holds, bidding four no trumps with the king of clubs, or signs off in the trump suit. Holding two kings the responder bids the higher-ranking of touching kings at the five-level, regarding all three side-suits as touching in a circle.

The opener may subsequently bid four no trumps or five clubs to ask the responder to show queens in similar fashion. Here is an example.

♠ A K Q J 7 6 3	♠ 8 4	*W*	*E*
♡ A K 3	♡ Q 7 6	2 ♣	2 ◇
◇ —	◇ 9 8 7 4 2	3 ♠	3 NT
♣ A K 7	♣ Q 6 4	4 ♣	4 ♠
		4 NT	6 ♣
		7 ♠	—

East shows scattered values with his second bid of three no trumps but denies a king in response to four clubs. His jump to six clubs on the next round shows the queens of both clubs and hearts and makes West a happy man.

Let us give the responder a different hand.

♠ A K Q J 7 6 3	♠ 8 4	*W*	*E*
♡ A K 3	♡ Q 7 6	2 ♣	2 ◇
◇ —	◇ A 8 7 4 2	3 ♠	4 ◇
♣ A K 7	♣ 9 6 4	4 NT	5 ♡
		7 NT	—

The bid of four no trumps clearly asks for queens in this case, for in view of the negative response to two clubs East cannot have a king as well as the ace already shown.

When the opener's suit is a minor, the jump carries the bidding to the four-level and space becomes cramped. The Sharples brothers therefore reverse the normal procedure, cue-bidding kings immediately over the jump and bidding four no trumps with any ace. In certain cases there may still be room to check on queens.

♠ A K 6	♠ Q 9 3	*W*	*E*
♡ A	♡ 10 8 7 4	2 ♣	2 ◇
◇ A 7	◇ K 6 5 4	4 ♣	4 ◇
♣ A K Q J 6 4 3	♣ 9 7	4 NT	5 ♠
		7 NT	—

This is a handy gadget to have at your command, although the opportunity to use it will not turn up very often.

Two Clubs on Shaded Values

By tradition the opening bid of two clubs is forcing to game with the exception of the following sequence.

	W	*E*
	2 ♣	2 ◇
	2 NT	

Here the opener shows a balanced hand with 23-24 points. The responder is expected to bid on with a queen and a jack but may pass with less.

Over the past decade, however, groups of players here and there have been insisting on further exceptions to the game-forcing principle. A contributing factor has been the adoption by many players of the Roman or Blue Club two diamond opening bid, which made it necessary to find an alternative method of dealing with strong diamond hands. Strong club hands have always been a bit of a problem, and one solution for minor suit hands containing nine or ten playing tricks is to open two clubs but allow the bidding to die at the four-level when responder has a blank hand.

♠ A K	*W*	*E*
♡ 7	2 ♣	2 ◇
◇ K Q J 9 8 6 2	3 ◇	3 ♠
♣ A 7 3	4 ◇	

At this point East is permitted to pass.

```
♠ 5                        W    E
♡ 9 4                      2 ♣  2 ♢
♢ A K 8                    3 ♣  3 ♡
♣ A K Q J 7 6 5            4 ♣
```

Again East may pass if he judges his hand to be worthless.

Some players carry the principle further, stipulating that the minimum rebid of a major suit by the opener should also be droppable. This treatment is incorporated in the Kaplan-Sheinwold system, where the standard for the opening bid of two clubs is lower than is normal.

```
♠ A Q 7                    W    E
♡ A Q J 10 5 4 2           2 ♣  2 ♢
♢ A 9 5                    2 ♡  2 NT
♣ —                        3 ♡
```

East may pass if unable to help.

For those who use weak two-bids in the major suits and cannot open such hands with an intermediate or Acol two-bid, this treatment has much to commend it. A big disadvantage of the two-club opening bid in the past has been its low frequency of occurrence. Relaxing the standard increases the frequency of the bid and at the same time limits the opening bid of one in a suit within a narrower and more effective range.

The last point is important if we are to hold our own against one-club systems, which enjoy their greatest advantage in dealing with hands in the 17-21 point range. By nibbling away at the top end of the range, two-club players can reduce this advantage.

Much recent thinking has been influenced by the proven success of the Italian one-club systems. Asking themselves why the devil should have all the best tunes, two-club players in many parts of the world have been experimenting with one feature in particular, the artificial step responses used in the Neapolitan and Blue Club style.

Step Responses to Two Clubs

There is nothing new in the idea of showing controls immediately in response to an opening bid of two clubs. For years CAB enthusiasts in Britain and many players in France have used the ace-showing responses devised by the great Pierre Albarran. But these are basically natural responses, although denoting aces rather than suits. The CAB schedule of responses is as follows.

> With an ace—bid the ace suit (three diamonds with the ace of diamonds).
> With two aces—bid three no trumps.
> With eight points including two kings—bid two no trumps.
> Lacking such values—bid two diamonds.

It might be thought hazardous to have to start showing genuine suits at the three-level or four-level, but devotees of the method claim that this is nothing compared to the advantage of hearing about the ace-content immediately. Mind you, CAB players are fortified by the knowledge that their two-club bids are never shaded, being unconditionally forcing to game.

Artificial step responses in the Neapolitan style are a fairly recent development, however. These work well after an opening bid of one club, so why not after two clubs? The bidding starts at a higher level, but on many hands it must be invaluable for the two-club bidder to learn at once the number of aces and kings held by his partner.

An ace is counted as two controls and a king as one, and there are two popular schedules of responses. The first, used by Edgar Kaplan and incorporated with slight modification by the Australians into the New South Wales system, is as follows.

$$2 \diamondsuit — 0 \text{ or } 1 \text{ control}$$
$$2 \heartsuit — 1 \text{ ace}$$
$$2 \spadesuit — 2 \text{ kings}$$
$$2 \text{ NT} — 3 \text{ kings}$$
$$3 \clubsuit — 1 \text{ ace and } 1 \text{ king}$$
$$3 \diamondsuit — 4 \text{ controls}$$

This schedule gives excellent definition, but it rises a little too steeply for comfort. In particular the two spade response, which compels the opener to rebid at the three-level, is unattractive when no more than two kings are held. Many players therefore prefer the alternative schedule, developed by Lawrence Rosler and Roger Stern in the United States and independently elsewhere.

2 ◇ — 0 or 1 control
2 ♡ — 2 controls
2 ♠ — 1 ace and 1 king
2 NT— 3 kings
3 ♣ — 4 controls
3 ◇ — 5 controls

There will occasionally be some ambiguity in the two heart response, but more often than not the opener will be able to tell by reference to his own hand whether his partner is showing an ace or two kings. When he cannot tell, he has ways of finding out.

It is useful to keep the distinction between responding hands containing an ace and a king and those with three kings, however. For one thing this ensures that the responder plays in no trumps only when he has genuine stoppers in three suits.

Taking this schedule of step responses as a base, I propose to outline an integrated method of slam bidding after an opening bid of two clubs.

2 ◇ *Response*—The bidding may stop below game when the opener shows limited values.

2 ♡ *Response* (2 controls)—Forcing to game.

2 ♠ *Response* (ace and king)—Forcing to game, and the responder must be wary of making a game bid when he has extra values.

2 *NT Response* (3 kings)—Forcing to 4 NT.

3 ♣ *Response* (4 controls)—Forcing to 4 NT.

3 ◇ *Response* (5 controls)—Forcing to slam.

3 ♡ *and* 3 ♠ *Responses*—Taking another leaf out of the Neapolitan book, we can play these as natural responses showing a good six-card suit and not more than one control. Since the level is higher than in Neapolitan the suit must be better. Six cards headed by the king and queen should be the standard.

3 *NT Response*—This can be used to show six controls, if you should be so lucky.

Opener's Rebid

After the step response the opener makes his natural rebid. With a balanced hand and 23-24 points he makes a minimum rebid in no trumps. With 25 or more points he jumps in no trumps. This is necessary to enable the responder to assess any extra values he may have.

♠ A K Q 5	♠ 7 4	W	E
♡ K Q 6	♡ A J 2	2 ♣	2 ♠
◇ A 10 3	◇ K Q 9 6 2	3 NT	5 NT
♣ A K J	♣ 8 7 3	7 NT	—

On hearing the jump rebid East knows the hands to be on the fringe of the grand slam zone. He issues an invitation which West is quick to accept.

With an unbalanced hand the opener bids his longest suit on the second round. The responder raises with three-card support, bids a five-card suit of his own, or bids no trumps. A jump rebid by responder indicates a solid or semi-solid six-card suit that is playable opposite a void.

Here the responder indicates ♠ K Q J 10 x x, a better suit than a first-round jump to three spades would have shown.

Asking on the Third Round

If ever there is a case for using asking bids, the ideal occasion is after an opening bid of two clubs. Cue-bidding is of dubious value in this situation. The opener normally has too many controls to show and the responder is unable to make an intelligent assessment.

Let us therefore stipulate that after suit agreement (whether direct, inferential or preferential) a further suit bid by the opener is an asking bid. Since the opener may wish to query third-round as well as other controls, the Precision type of asking bid seems best suited to our method. The schedule of responses is repeated here for convenience.

1st step — no control in asked suit
2nd step — queen or doubleton
3rd step — king or singleton
4th step — ace or void
5th step — AK

A repeat asking bid demands further clarification. I like to add a third and fourth step to the responses for use only when the responder has shown the ace or king.

1st step — control by shortage
2nd step — control by high card
3rd step — ace or king singleton or doubleton
4th step — A Q x (x) (x) or K Q x (x) (x)

The repeat asking bid can also be used after a negative response to query the responder's length in the suit.

1st step — three cards only
2nd step — four or more cards

The opener who holds a self-sufficient suit can start an asking sequence by making a jump rebid in his suit. This sets the trump suit, demands a relay bid from the responder, and promises an asking bid on the next round. Naturally in such cases the responder must not show voids, singletons or doubletons unless he has at least a couple of trumps.

W	E
2 ♣	2 ♡ (two controls)
3 ♠ (trumps)	3 NT (relay)
4 ◇ (asking bid)	

To make an asking bid agreeing the responder's suit, the opener must normally jump.

W	E
2 ♣	2 ♡
3 ◇	3 ♠
5 ♣ (asking bid, agreeing spades)	

After a rebid in no trumps, however, the opener can agree the responder's suit without jumping.

W	E
2 ♣	2 ♠
2 NT	3 ♡
4 ♣ (asking bid, agreeing hearts)	

West would rebid three no trumps to deny three-card support, hence any suit bid agrees hearts and asks.

Four No Trumps

This is not needed for the normal purpose of checking on aces and kings. After trump agreement four no trumps by the opener is best used as an enquiry for queens. Here is a workable schedule of responses.

5 ♣ — no queen
5 ◇ — minor suit queen
5 ♡ — major suit queen
5 ♠ — two queens of same rank or colour
5 NT— two queens of different rank and colour
6 ♣ — three queens

A jump to four no trumps would, of course, agree the responder's suit as well as asking for queens.

Five No Trumps

A jump to five no trumps can be used as the grand slam force in cases where 4 NT will not infallibly give the answer. A bid of 5 NT without a jump, however, is reserved to ask for extra trump length. Minimum trump length is defined as follows.

When responder has supported   — 3 cards
When responder has bid the suit   — 5 cards
When responder has jumped in the suit— 6 cards

In response to a trump length query of 5 NT:

6 ♣ — shows minimum length
6 ◇ — shows one extra trump
and so on.

Let us have a look at some examples and see how the method works.

♠ K Q 8 7 6 3	♠ A J 9	W	E
♡ A	♡ K 7 2	2 ♣	2 ♠
◇ A K 4	◇ 6 5 2	3 ♠	4 ♣
♣ A K 6	♣ 8 7 5 4	4 NT?	5 ♣
		5 ◇ ?	5 ♡
		6 ♣ ?	6 ◇
		6 NT	—

After the first round of bidding West knows that all the aces and kings are present. On hearing about spade support he asks for queens with 4 NT. This produces a negative response and West sets about discovering what he can of his partner's distribution. When East denies a doubleton in either minor suit West knows that a grand slam cannot be a good bet.

Using standard methods West might well gamble on finding a thirteenth trick in his partner's hand.

♠ A K Q J 5	♠ 10 4	W	E
♡ K Q J 7	♡ A 9 3	2 ♣	2 ♠
◇ A 6 3	◇ K 5	3 ♠	4 ♣
♣ A	♣ J 10 7 6 4 2	4 ♡	4 ♠
		4 NT?	5 ♣
		5 ◇?	5 NT
		6 ◇?	6 NT
		7 ♠	—

Having dragged a spade preference from his partner, West checks on queens before asking in diamonds and hearing about second-round control. The repeat ask discovers that the diamond control is the king singleton or doubleton, which makes the grand slam a good proposition. West would also have bid the grand slam if his partner had shown a singleton diamond (and therefore the king of clubs), but if East had denied third-round diamond control West would have settled for six no trumps.

♠ A	♠ Q J 9 6 4	W	E
♡ A K Q J 8 7 3 2	♡ 6	2 ♣	2 ♡
◇ K 5	◇ A Q 7	4 ♡	4 ♠
♣ A 2	♣ 9 7 4 3	5 ◇?	6 ♣
		6 ◇?	7 ♣
		7 NT	—

The jumps to four hearts sets the trump suit and demands a relay of four spades. West asks twice in diamonds and discovers East to have three or more cards headed by the ace and queen.

♠ K	♠ A Q J 10 4 3	W	E
♡ A Q 10 6 5	♡ 7 2	2 ♣	2 ♠
◇ A K Q 3	◇ 9 8 4	3 ♡	4 ♠
♣ A Q 5	♣ K 6	7 NT	—

This is a simple hand for the method. Once West hears about the semi-solid six-card suit he can count thirteen tricks no matter where his partner's king lies.

♠ A 6	♠ 9 5 4	W	E
♡ A K 7 2	♡ J 8 6 5 4 3	2 ♣	2 ♡
♢ K Q 4	♢ A 8	2 NT	3 ♡
♣ A K 5 2	♣ Q 6	4 ♣?	4 ♡
		5 ♣?	5 ♡
		5 NT?	6 ♢
		7 NT	—

West agrees his partner's suit by asking in clubs. The response promises third-round control, and on the next round East confirms that this is the queen. Finally West checks on trump length and counts to thirteen when his partner shows a six-carder.

♠ A Q 9	♠ 8 6 3	W	E
♡ A K J 6 5	♡ Q 4	2 ♣	2 ♢
♢ A	♢ 10 8 7	2 ♡	3 ♣
♣ A K 4 2	♣ Q J 8 7 5	4 NT?	5 NT
		7 ♣	—

West jumps to four no trumps, agreeing clubs and asking for queens. The five no trump response shows just the right cards for the grand slam.

The most difficult slam auctions are those in which the wrong suit is agreed at an early stage. The repeat asking bid after a negative response will sometimes indicate the need to change horses.

♠ A 6	♠ J 9 3	W	E
♡ A K Q 9 6 3	♡ 10 8 5 4	2 ♣	2 ♢
♢ 5	♢ 8 2	2 ♡	3 ♡
♣ A K Q J	♣ 9 8 7 5	3 ♠?	3 NT
		4 ♣?	4 ♢
		5 ♣?	5 ♡
		6 ♣	—

After receiving a negative response to his asking bid in spades West does not give up, for he realises that a slam may yet be on if his partner has four clubs. The repeated asking bids disclose the fit and the slam is duly bid.

If we alter the responding hand we can see another way in which a repeat ask after a negative response can bring good results.

		W	E
♠ A 6	♠ 7 5 4	2 ♣	2 ◇
♡ A K Q 9 6 3	♡ 10 8 4 3	2 ♡	3 ♡
◇ 5	◇ J 8 3 2	3 ♠?	3 NT
♣ A K Q J	♣ 9 5	4 ♣?	4 ♡
		4 ♠?	4 NT
		6 ♡	—

After discovering the doubleton club, West makes a repeat ask in spades and finds his partner with precisely three cards in the suit. The slam now becomes a fair proposition. Even if East has only three trumps, the suit may break 2-2 or the opponent with three trumps may have to follow to four rounds of clubs.

		W	E
♠ A K Q 7	♠ 8 6	2 ♣	2 ♡
♡ A	♡ 10 8 4	3 ◇	4 ◇
◇ A K J 6 5	◇ 10 9 7 4 3	4 NT?	5 ♣
♣ K 6 4	♣ A 7 3	5 ♡?	5 ♠
		5 NT?	6 ♡
		7 ◇	—

Once the diamonds are supported West decides to commit himself to slam. The enquiry for queens meets with a negative response, but West probes for distributional values with an asking bid in hearts. On hearing that his partner has at least three cards in the suit, West realises that it is safe to make one more try with five no trumps. The response reveals the five-card support that makes the grand slam a good contract.

		W	E
♠ A 10 7 3	♠ K 9 8 6 4 2	2 ♣	2 ♡
♡ A 4	♡ K 10 2	2 NT	3 ♠
◇ A K J	◇ 8 4	4 ♣?	4 ♡
♣ A K 8 3	♣ 6 5	4 NT?	5 ♣
		5 ◇?	5 ♠
		5 NT?	6 ◇
		7 ♠	—

On learning about his partner's spade suit West unleashes a

series of asking bids, discovering that East has no queens but doubletons in both minor suits. Finally West checks on trump length and bids the grand slam when East admits to a sixth spade.

From these examples it is clear that the method can be effective in searching out the features needed for a grand slam, but you must not expect to solve all your problems by adopting control-showing responses to two clubs plus asking bids.

After experimenting with the method for six months I have found the step responses to be unsatisfactory in several respects. When a fit is quickly established all goes smoothly, but when no fit is apparent the machinery tends to grind, especially when the step response coincides with the opener's long suit. Consider the following example.

♠ A Q 9 6 3	♠ 7 2	W	E
♡ Q	♡ K 10 9 5 3	2 ♣	2 ♠
◊ A K Q J	◊ 9 4	3 ♠	4 ♡
♣ K Q 6	♣ A 8 4 3	?	

The optimum contract has been left behind and the bidding is not yet over. The best that West can hope for is to be allowed to play in four spades, although even that may be too high if the cards are unkind. If West attempts to find a fit by bidding his second suit he is almost bound to end up with a minus score.

Note that the hands present no problem for standard methods. The bidding would normally proceed:

W	E		W	E
2 ♣	2 ♡	or	2 ♣	2 ♡
2 ♠	3 ♣		2 ♠	3 ♣
3 NT	—		3 ◊	3 NT

A further disadvantage of the step responses is the lack of a genuine negative. A response of two diamonds has to be made on quite powerful hands when the requisite two controls are not held, and it may be difficult for the responder to catch up in the later bidding. One might get around the problem by adopting the Blue Club style of using the diamond response for "bust" hands and the heart response for hands with six or more points. But half the advantage of the method is lost if the heart response no longer guarantees two controls.

Here is the sort of unwieldy "negative" response that poses problems in the step method.

♠ A K 9 5	♠ Q J 10 3	W	E
♡ A	♡ Q J 9 8 2	2 ♣	2 ◇
◇ 8 7	◇ K Q 5	3 ♣	3 ♡
♣ A K Q J 6 5	♣ 3	3 ♠	5 ♠
		?	

What is West to do? He will probably pass, expecting his partner's main values to be in hearts rather than diamonds. East might have gambled on the slam himself, but that would not have been a success if his partner's heart and diamond holdings had been reversed.

It is hard to imagine the slam being missed if East is able to make a natural positive response of two hearts.

Natural Responses with Asking Bids

In view of the difficulties experienced with step responses, some players who wish to brighten up their two-club sequences may prefer to use natural responses in conjunction with asking bids. These fit together quite well. On the last example the bidding would go:

W	E
2 ♣	2 ♡
3 ♣	3 ♠
5 ◇?	5 NT
6 ♠	—

One advantage of natural responses is that they allow room for a Precision-type trump asking bid on the second round. This comes into operation when the opener raises the responder's suit.

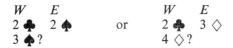

W	E		W	E
2 ♣	2 ♠	or	2 ♣	3 ◇
3 ♠?			4 ◇?	

In each case West is asking about the length and quality of East's trumps. One possible schedule of responses is the following:

1st step — 4 trumps with ace or king
2nd step — 4 trumps with two top honours

3rd step — 5 or 6 trumps with no top honour
4th step — 5 or 6 trumps with one top honour
5th step — 5 or 6 trumps with two top honours
6th step — three top honours

The failure to distinguish between five and six-card length at this stage is not too important, since 5 NT is still available as a check on trump length. Players who do not care to bid four-card suits in response to two clubs, however, can start with five or six small trumps as their first step and build up from there.

Here is an example of the trump asking bid.

♠ A K 4	♠ 8 7 2	W	E
♡ K 7 6 5	♡ A Q 9 4 2	2 ♣	2 ♡
◇ A	◇ Q 8 5	3 ♡?	4 ♡
♣ A K J 10 5	♣ Q 6	4 ♠?	4 NT
		5 ♣?	5 ♡
		6 ♣?	6 ♡
		7 NT	—

Having discovered his partner to hold five hearts headed by two top honours and the queen of clubs, West can count thirteen tricks.

After a natural response to two clubs the opener will have to work rather harder to discover the controls held by his partner. Asking bids can do the job, but they will need to be selected with care to avoid wasting bidding space.

The four no trump enquiry for queens has to be abandoned, since four no trumps is now needed to check on aces and kings. The schedule of responses from page 123 is repeated here for convenience.

Response to 4 NT	After negative response to 2 ♣	After positive response to 2 ♣
5 ♣ —	no controls	K
5 ◇ —	K	KK
5 ♡ —	KK	A plus
5 ♠ —	A	AK or KKK
5 NT —	A plus	AA, AKK or KKKK

These responses to 4 NT give information similar to that obtained from the step responses to two clubs. The main difference is the level. Here is an example of the method.

The five-diamond response to four no trumps shows two kings, and after confirming that one of these is not the king of clubs West bids the grand slam. Step responses to two clubs would, of course, work equally well on this hand.

The methods presented in this chapter have not been exhaustively tested and there is obviously scope for further research. But I can promise that anyone who cares to experiment with asking bids after two clubs, in conjunction with either natural or step responses, will have a lot of fun.

12 · Special Slam Tries

In this final chapter my intention is to tie up one or two loose ends and examine some ideas for slam tries in unusual situations. When the bidding starts in a way that does not normally suggest slam possibilities, the holder of a big hand is apt to find himself at a loss unless he has special weapons at his disposal.

After Pre-emption

The opening pre-emptive bid in first or second position is fine for obstructive purposes, but it can have a boomerang effect if the responder has a strong hand. At the three-level there may be enough room for manoeuvre. After an opening bid of four hearts or four spades, however, the responder is left with no safety margin. A random cue-bid is unlikely to produce a satisfactory result, since the opener will not know what his partner is looking for.

Bob and Jim Sharples, who over the years have developed a bid for just about every situation under the sun, suggest the following solution to the problem.

After an opening bid of four hearts or four spades, a responder strong enough to envisage a slam should make his cue-bid in the suit immediately below that in which he requires a control from his partner. This device is really no more than a matter of common sense, but it can do no harm to formalize it by partnership agreement.

Naturally the responder will not be interested in making a slam try when he lacks control in two side suits. He will invariably be concerned about one particular suit, and his cue-bid in the suit below enables the opener to co-operate intelligently. Holding second-round control in the suit above the cue-bid, the opener can safely bid the slam unless his trumps are unusually weak.

Here are some examples.

♠ 9 4	♠ A K Q J 5	W	E
♡ A J 10 8 7 6 3 2	♡ K 4	4 ♡	5 ♣
◇ 6	◇ 10 5 3	6 ♡	—
♣ 7 5	♣ A 8 2		

East makes his cue-bid in clubs and West bids the slam on the strength of his diamond control.

♠ K Q J 9 8 7 5 2	♠ A 3	W	E
♡ 2	♡ A K J 6	4 ♠	5 ♡
◇ 8 7	◇ A Q 9 4	5 ♠	—
♣ 8 3	♣ Q 6 4		

Lacking the required club control, West has to sign off in five spades.

When holding first-round control in the suit above his partner's cue-bid, the opener will naturally make a cue-bid himself.

♠ A K J 9 7 6 3	♠ Q 5 2	W	E
♡ —	♡ J 9 4 3	4 ♠	5 ◇
◇ J 10 7 4	◇ A K	5 ♡	5 NT
♣ 7 6	♣ A K Q 5	7 ♠	—

On hearing that there are no heart losers East is able to introduce the grand slam force.

This idea can be extended for use after sequences such as 2 NT-4 ♡ and 2 NT-4 ♠, where the responder's jump is regarded by many players as a mild slam try.

♠ Q 10 7 4	♠ 8	W	E
♡ A 8 4	♡ K Q 10 9 6 3	2 NT	4 ♡
◇ A K 5	◇ J 10 4	5 ◇	6 ♡
♣ A K 7	♣ Q 10 6 2		

West makes his cue-bid in diamonds and East knows that his spade control is what is needed.

After Three No Trumps

Reverting to the subject of pre-emptive bids, we take a look next at the gambling three no trump opening bid. As it is generally played today, this opening indicates a solid six or seven-card minor suit without as much as a king in outside strength. An idea developed by Terence Reese in connection with his Little Major system is well worth adding to the repertoire.

Reese suggests that a response of four diamonds be used as an enquiry for singletons. With no singleton the opener signs off in four no trumps. With a singleton heart or spade he names the suit, and with a singleton in the other minor he bids his long suit. This can give valuable information to the responder.

♠ Q 5	♠ A 7	W	E
♡ 8 7 3	♡ A K Q J 5	3 NT	4 ◇
◇ A K Q J 7 5 4	◇ 10 8	5 ◇	6 ◇
♣ 8	♣ Q 10 9 3		

East is prepared to play in four no trumps but gladly bids the slam in diamonds when he hears about his partner's singleton club.

After the Acol Two

In the Acol style an opening bid of two in a major suit indicates a powerful hand with at least eight playing tricks. Traditionally, a single raise by the responder promises an ace, while a double raise indicates an ace-less hand normally containing two second-round controls. This double raise is valuable in a negative sense, but when the opener has good controls he is left with little space for slam exploration.

If the opener merely needs to know the number of kings held by his partner he can bid four no trumps to find out. But when he needs to know about a specific second-round control, his best action is not clearly defined in standard methods.

As usual, the Sharples brothers have a bid to fit the occasion. They play that the bid of a new suit by the opener enquires directly for controls in that suit. Holding both second and third-round control, the responder goes straight to slam.

♠ A K 9 8 7 6 3	♠ Q 5 4 2	W	E
♡ A K	♡ J 9 4 3	2 ♠	4 ♠
◇ —	◇ K Q 7 6	5 ♣	6 ♠
♣ J 10 6 2	♣ 7		

Holding only second-round control in the vital suit, the

responder may, when space permits, make a waiting bid in another suit.

♠ A K J 5	♠ 9 4	W	E
♡ A K 8 6 4 3 2	♡ J 9 7 5	2 ♡	4 ♡
◇ —	◇ K 8 7 4	5 ♣	5 ◇
♣ Q 7	♣ K 6 2	6 ♡	—

East's second bid of five diamonds expresses doubt about the quality of his club control, but for West any club control is good enough.

♠ A K Q 8 7 6	♠ J 10 3	W	E
♡ —	♡ K J 8 3	2 ♠	4 ♠
◇ A 7 6 4 3	◇ K 8 2	5 ◇	5 ♡
♣ K Q	♣ 10 9 5	5 ♠	—

This time the insecure diamond control is not enough, for West has two losers staring him in the face.

Clearly the Sharples method will often prove superior to asking bids, for in such situations there is no room for a repeat asking bid. Nevertheless, Precision asking bids will do a reasonable job and will serve to locate third-round control when this is all that is required.

♠ K J 10 9 6 4 3	♠ Q 8 2	W	E
♡ A	♡ K 9 8 5	2 ♠	4 ♠
◇ A K 7 6 2	◇ 8 2	5 ◇?	5 ♠
♣ —	♣ K Q 7 4	6 ♠	—

West can bid the slam when he hears about third-round diamond control.

After a single raise of an Acol two-bid, asking bids can be equally useful. Here is a hand from the Lederer inter-club team contest of 1969 on which only one pair out of eight managed to reach the lay-down grand slam

♠ A Q 9 7 5 4 3	♠ K J 10 8 6
♡ K 9 7 3	♡ A 4
◇ A	◇ 10 7 3
♣ A	♣ 10 6 5

It is a tricky hand for cue-bidders in that it is not easy for East to appreciate that his third-round heart control is the key feature.

The modified responses to Precision asking bids can reveal the position, however.

W	E
2 ♠	3 ♠
4 ♡?	5 ◇
5 ♡?	6 ♣
6 ♡?	7 ♠

East's response to the repeat asking bid shows that his ace is singleton or doubleton. West then uses the Baron slam try to query the quality of his partner's trumps, and East has no hesitation in bidding the grand slam.

On the next hand a cold grand slam was missed at both tables in the British final trials of 1963.

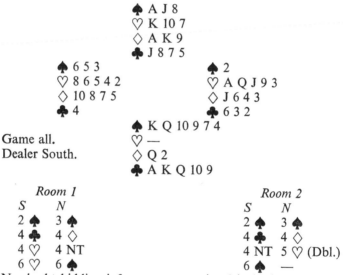

```
                    ♠ A J 8
                    ♡ K 10 7
                    ◇ A K 9
                    ♣ J 8 7 5
        ♠ 6 5 3              ♠ 2
        ♡ 8 6 5 4 2          ♡ A Q J 9 3
        ◇ 10 8 7 5           ◇ J 6 4 3
        ♣ 4                  ♣ 6 3 2
                    ♠ K Q 10 9 7 4
Game all.           ♡ —
Dealer South.       ◇ Q 2
                    ♣ A K Q 10 9
```

Room 1		Room 2	
S	N	S	N
2 ♠	3 ♠	2 ♠	3 ♠
4 ♣	4 ◇	4 ♣	4 ◇
4 ♡	4 NT	4 NT	5 ♡ (Dbl.)
6 ♡	6 ♠	6 ♠	—

No doubt bidding inferences were missed in both rooms, but the fact remains that two of the best pairs in the country failed to reach a simple grand slam.

The Precision asking sequence allows little scope for errors of judgement.

The response to the asking bid in diamonds shows the ace and king, and the response to the trump asking bid shows one top honour.

When Opponents Open

So far the opponents have been remarkably quiet, and I do not propose to allow them to become too active even now. Competitive slam bidding, which is often sacrificial in nature, is a matter of judgement rather than technique and is beyond the scope of this book.

Nevertheless, the opponents do at times open the bidding when there is a cold slam on for our side, and it is important to have some machinery to deal with this problem. In the past a strong attacking hand, particularly a two-suiter, was shown by making an immediate cue-bid in the enemy suit. This treatment has been abandoned by many tournament players, who now use the immediate cue-bid in second position as Michaels, showing a weak distributional hand. It thus becomes necessary to find an adequate substitute for the strong cue-bid.

One way in which this can be done is by taking another leaf from the Roman book.

Roman Jump Overcalls

In the Roman system a jump overcall in a suit shows a two-suited hand, specifying the suit bid and the next higher-ranking unbid suit. If the opening bid is one heart, for instance, an overcall of two spades shows spades and clubs, three clubs shows clubs and diamonds, and three diamonds shows diamonds and spades.

At least five cards are guaranteed in each of the suits, and the normal strength for the bid is 11-15 points with five or six losers in the hand.

Naturally the Roman jump overcall does not often lead to a

slam contract. For slam purposes we have to enlist the aid of its big brother, the jump overcall of two no trumps.

Roman 2 NT Overcall

The jump overcall of two no trumps shows a powerful two-suiter with no more than four losers. Partner is required to make an automatic relay bid in the lower unbid minor—normally clubs. The overcaller reveals his hand as follows. When the relay suit is one of his suits he bids the other; when he does not hold the relay suit he bids no trumps.

S	W	N	E
1 ♣	2 NT	—	3 ◇
—	3 NT	—	

Thus on the above sequence East is required to choose between the major suits.

This jump overcall of two no trumps makes an ideal substitute for the strong cue-bid in second position. Nothing is lost, since strong balanced hands can double on the first round and follow up with a bid of two no trumps. If you are playing Roman jump overcalls, of course, you have no need for the two no trump overcall in an "unusual" sense.

The adoption of Roman jump overcalls involves the loss of the strong jump overcall used in standard methods to show a one-suited hand. On such hands you have to double and bid the suit on the next round, but this is no great hardship.

Those who favour weak jump overcalls are invariably aggressive players who like to interfere with the enemy bidding whenever possible. They will find that they can do this even more effectively by adopting the Roman two-suited version.

Returning to our theme of slam bidding, let us have a look at a hand from the 1972 Team Olympiad at Miami. The competitors found it hard to envisage a grand slam on a combined total of 22 high-card points. Most stopped in game, four hearts doubled and made being a popular result.

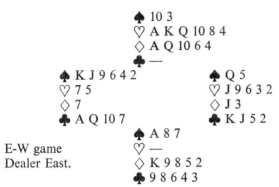

♠ 10 3
♡ A K Q 10 8 4
♢ A Q 10 6 4
♣ —

♠ K J 9 6 4 2   ♠ Q 5
♡ 7 5   ♡ J 9 6 3 2
♢ 7   ♢ J 3
♣ A Q 10 7   ♣ K J 5 2

♠ A 8 7
♡ —
♢ K 9 8 5 2
♣ 9 8 6 4 3

E-W game
Dealer East.

The North hand is ideally suited for a Roman 2 NT overcall.
Here is a logical bidding sequence.

W	N	E	S
	—	—	—
1 ♠	2 NT	—	3 ♣
—	3 NT	—	4 ♢
—	5 ♣	—	5 ♠
—	5 NT	—	6 ♣
—	7 ♢	all pass	

Asked to choose between the red suits, South bids a quiet four
diamonds. On the way to game North takes the opportunity to
show his club control. When South cue-bids his ace of spades in
return, all that North has to do is to check on the king of trumps
before bidding the grand slam.

Jump Cue-Bid Overcall

For a number of years I have been using the Roman jump
cue-bid overcall (e.g. 1 ♠, 3 ♠ or 1 ♢, 3 ♢) to indicate a strong
three-suited hand, 4-4-4-1 or 5-4-4-0 in distribution with at least
17 high-card points in the three suits. It is, in fact, the sort of hand
that would open the bidding with a Roman 2 ♢. It can be
difficult to express this type of hand adequately after doubling on
the first round.

This jump cue-bid overcall may not come along very often, but
it can lead to good distributional slams when it does make an
appearance.

The responder can bid the enemy suit at the four-level to discover whether his partner has a singleton or a void in the suit. The overcaller bids his five-card suit if he has one, and otherwise bids four no trumps. Here is an example.

♠ A J 6 2	♠ Q 4	S	W	N	E
♡ —	♡ 9 8 4	1 ♡	3 ♡	—	4 ♡
◇ K Q 8 3	◇ A 7 6 5	—	5 ♣	—	6 ♣
♣ A K J 6 3	♣ Q 9 4 2	all pass			

If West had shown a 4-4-4-1 shape East would have been satisfied to play at the five-level, but the knowledge of the extra club and the void heart makes the slam seem a pretty good bet.

That brings us to the end of the chapter and the end of the book. At this stage I expect most readers to be afflicted by the mental indigestion that comes from examining a hundred different slam conventions within a short space of time. But remember that you don't have to play them all. Indeed you can't play them all, for there are many that are incompatible. The best plan is to make a careful choice from amongst those conventions best suited to your style. I hope that even those who disagree strongly with my views will have found something in these pages that will help them derive more profit and enjoyment from their slam bidding.

Index